Studies on the Chinese Market Economy Series

Several Issues Arising During the Retracking of the Chinese Economy

Chief Editors:
Gao Shangquan *and* Chi Fulin

FOREIGN LANGUAGES PRESS   BEIJING

First Edition 1997

The project is aided by
(Hainan) China Foundation for Reform and Development Research

ISBN 7-119-01976-7

© Foreign Languages Press, Beijing, 1997

Published by Foreign Languages Press
24 Baiwanzhuang Road, Beijing 100037, China

Distributed by China International Book Trading Corporation
35 Chegongzhuang Xilu, Beijing 100044, China
P.O. Box 399, Beijing, China

Printed in the People's Republic of China

FOREWORD

China is in a state of transition from a traditional planned economy to a socialist market economy. This transition is the most important event in China's recent history.

How to accelerate the pace of reform and smoothly make the transition from existing conditions to a market economy are the questions of the day.

During the past 20 years, reform of the Chinese economy has passed through several stages of development. New conditions and new problems continually arise requiring study and solution. At present, many of these problems demand broader thinking, uncompromising investigation and clear analysis in the search for optimum solutions. For instance, we have set as a goal the establishment of a modern enterprise system. So, how can we actually attain this goal? This requires the solutions to a series of deeply ingrained problems.

Major reform targets have been very clearly set in the recent period but many conflicts and contradictions have appeared which impede their implementation. This now has become a rather complicated situation.

Keeping in mind that the major goal of reform is the establishment of a market economy, we must now make a thorough and concrete study of various aspects of reform so that these obstacles can be removed.

China's socioeconomic development is now at a crucial stage. Can the economy sustain the current rapid rate of growth? It must be our goal to ensure that it does. The suggestions and ideas in the six chapters of this book try, insofar as possible, to meet this demand.

Chapter one, for example, puts forward concrete proposals for the reform of state-owned enterprises. These proposals proceed from the premise that a general solution is required to bring these enterprises back to life. On the subject of macroeconomic reform, in chapter two we have offered concrete suggestions for controlling inflation according to the principles of a market economy. Chapter three deals with the rural economy and how we can speed up rural market reform. In chapter four we focus our attention on solving the problem of the inconsistencies in regional development and on policies conducive to the further opening of developed regions. Chapter five deals with the introduction of a new social security system which stresses both the just and equitable treatment of individual staff and workers, and the overall efficiency of the system. Chpter six explores legislation, touching on the evolution of legislation in recent times and stressing that legislation is closely linked to the process of economic reform.

The author believes that in this reform period, in order to guarantee sustained and rapid economic growth, we must establish a market economic system.

My studies on reform in recent years, coupled with my opportunities to participate in research, have been invaluable in the formulation of the ideas presented in this book. I have been able to talk with many specialists and have benefited greatly from these discussions. My colleagues, Sun Xiuping and Zhu Huayou, have been an enormous help.

Economic reform is a very large topic and we must continue to give it serious attention.

My heartfelt thanks go to the many colleagues who have helped in the publication of this book, and in particular the (Hainan) China Foundation for Reform and Development Research for its support.

Chi Fulin
June 28, 1995

Contents

Chapter I
Reform of State-Owned Enterprises

The reform of state-owned enterprises plays the most decisive role in China's transition from a planned economy to a market economy. These enterprises have already gone through many changes over the past decade. But fusing them fully into the framework of a modern market economy presents problems which demand further bold exploration and confrontation. Many issues remain to be satisfactorily resolved, from basic theory to concrete practical application. Several years ago the author of this book proposed that state assets should enter the market and become market-oriented. The purpose of this proposal is to explore the most efficient methods of making the transition from state enterprise to state asset and market orientation. I wanted to find a way to stimulate and energize the state economy as a whole rather than concentrating on the handling of individual state enterprises. Some of my views, such as market orientation of state assets, were publicly criticized. It was thought I was advocating wholesale privatization. This was not the case and was a distortion of my intention.

The question is how to make reforms of state enterprises suit the needs of the market. And this calls for further deep investigation.

I. Energizing the Overall State Economy

A. The State-Owned Economy Should Provide a Leading Role in Overall Prosperity and Competitive Power

Under market economy conditions the reform of state-owned enterprises must be focused on achieving competitive power so as to enable state-owned assets to play a leading role in the national economy.

The most important problem here is how to speedily integrate these enterprises into the market economy and obtain maximum efficiency. If this problem is solved well, it will greatly accelerate the reform of both state enterprise and the government management system and enable state enterprises to take a leading role in the national economy.

As this transition progresses, state enterprises will realize increasing benefit and competitive power until they become a dominant force in the total capital of society, able to exercise control and influence over the national economy.

To do this, emphasis in state investments should change from ordinary competitive enterprises to basic industry and other strategic areas and professions. This, of course, does not mean that the operation of state assets should not be competitive. It does mean that:

1) the state assets will become very active in competitive professions and areas that bear directly on the national economy and people's standard of living.

2) the operation of state enterprises in basic industry and public utilities must be carried out so as to enhance the efficiency of and benefit to the state asset by successfully competing not only with non-government-owned enterprises but amongst each other.

3) the competition between state-owned assets in basic industry and public utilities should be carried out intelligently to avoid creating barriers between different departments and regions, diversified ownership, blind launching of projects and duplicative construction all of which lead to wastage of resources.

Assuming a leading role in a state-owned economy does not necessarily lie in absolute superiority of quantity nor in the concentration of all economic spheres into the hands of the state. In ordinary professions and industry government owned enterprise can compete with the non-national sector on an equal footing and for mutual development. But in those spheres that affect the overall economy and standard of living the government owned enterprises should maintain control and fully manage quality and economic performance so as to ensure actual competitive power.

The superiority of state assets should come into full play in the careful planning of its allocation, organization and structure. Let state enterprises prosper or go out of existence in conformity with the principles of a market economy—fostering the good and scrapping the obsolete.

The three superiorities are as follows:

Allocation superiority—state asset stock should be placed under good management and handled well. As a result of a manager's effort the value of any state asset should be preserved and increased while its scale is expanded. State capital should be reinvested to further increase the strength of state assets.

Organizational superiority—this means firstly that state assets should be utilized to abundantly fund the projects and enterprises that have a major impact on the economy. Secondly, through the establishment of state holding companies nongovernmental assets and enterprises can be absorbed and placed under control in organized conglomerates.

Structural superiority—this means overall enhancement of the national economy by fostering an optimum organization of state assets. This includes reduction of loss-making state enterprises. In this way state assets will play an ever increasing role in the control and guiding of the national economy. They will be used to guarantee investment to those sectors which will most benefit the national economy and, as needed, to shore up any weak links.

To deepen the reform of state enterprises market competition should be encouraged to develop enterprises that do have superiority. Assets and resources will then be transferred to those enterprises which have demonstrated the highest efficiency thereby enhancing the vitality of the entire national economy. We must not let it be thought that before state assets can assume a leading role in the economy that every state enterprise need be energized and on an upswing. This is neither possible nor necessary in fact. As the social insurance system becomes established, state enterprises that have been making losses for long periods of time, with liabilities exceeding assets, and which show no signs or prospect of recovery, should gradually be allowed to declare themselves bankrupt. Where possible other individuals or corporations can be allowed to merge with or buy out these enterprises. Any remaining assets should be sold by public auction. In the case of small state enterprises they can be leased or bought as the case may be. As for enterprises which have achieved a superior position in the market economy, from the point of view of policy, they should be rewarded. They can evolve into principal enterprises which can become the mainstay of the national economy. Of course, priority should be given to big enterprises or enterprise groups which have the strongest bearing on national economy and standard of living. This includes those involved in both domestic and in international markets as well as those which accelerate China's industrialization.

B. Ensuring Optimum Conservation of State Assets

This is a problem of great and practical significance that has to be solved in the transition from planned to market economy. It's not just a problem of guaranteeing or increasing the value of state assets in the ordinary sense of the word. Its aim is to give a correct definition of the position and function of state assets in a socialist market economy. In the old days under the planned economy system, state enterprise encompassed almost every sphere and aspect of society's economic life. This had two direct consequences: total efficiency of state enterprises was extremely low and state assets were ineffectively and inadequately being utilized. We have noted the problem of conserving and increasing the value of state assets during this period of reform. This is entirely necessary for no matter what the circumstances, the increase or decrease in the value of state assets is a vital consideration—they must not be allowed to devalue, expire, or go to waste. However, in the course of the economy's transition, it is woefully inadequate to worry only about immediately increases. We must seriously study and determine the best overall utilization of these assets for both the immediate and long term interests of the national economy. We must study and solve the problem of how to best use these assets to readjust and control the market economy and create an adequate environment and infrastructure which will guarantee China's sustained, speedy and stable economic development.

In doing this we are using a concept far more embracive than merely conserving and increasing the value of state assets—important as these may be. We must seek to use state assets to achieve the maximum long term benefit to the national economy and to the entire society as well.

This "optimum benefit of state asset" is a demand of any socialist market economy in the course of its development. The mark of a market economy is the competition between economic entities in their pursuit of maximum profit. As can be seen this can easily deteriorate into fixations on economics that bring in high profit quickly and in short cycles while neglecting economic projects that bring in profit slowly and involve longer cycles. Doubtless it is true that the market economy itself contains contradictions between partial and whole interest, immediate and long term profits, and personal and social benefits. Yet a socialist market economy calls for speedy, embracive, sustained, stable and harmonious development of the entire national economy. This requires the state to use its abundant material resources to create conditions which force the development of priority areas and to take the large scale actions necessary to enable the large state enterprises to successfully participate in the market economy so as to positively influence the economy's development. This would include the use of state assets to handle the above mentioned inherent contradictions in a market economy.

Thus we see that the role of state assets in the betterment of the economy can not be overstated. When they are employed in the direction of long term stable development they bring better results: they impact on the economy as a whole and also guarantee long term expansion of assets and a wider and more stable economic base.

Under modern market economy conditions we must stress

conserving and increasing the value of state assets. We must stress even more, however, the employment of these state assets to strengthen the economy's long term capital base.

In considering the optimum use of state assets we must readjust our orientation as to its best investment. Viewed from the standpoint of overall social benefit, national economic growth, or optimum long term development it is clear that the power of state assets manifests best when injected into basic industry, emerging new industry, or community social services.

A vital function of the correct use of state assets lies in the development of infrastructure and the organization of basic industry. These two factors determine, in large measure, the long term development of the economy as a whole. At present the serious lag in China's industrial and agricultural infrastructure is inhibiting the development and adaptation of basic industry to the needs of the national economy. This constraint is an outstanding problem and should be tackled by large scale infusions of state funds into infrastructure and basic industry. This in turn will lay a firm foundation for future development.

As we implement a socialist market economy state assets should and must occupy the main position and play the leading role in such fields as banking, insurance, postal-communications, and aero-space.

Although there sometimes may be economic conflicts in funding social programs, their overall benefits to society outweigh any such problems. State assets are obliged to fund these programs. At present, advancement of China's social services, public utilities, education and cultural works is lagging behind, being unable to keep pace with the current need and demand. In the interests of the entire society more investments should be gradually made to augment these fields.

Optimum use of state assets requires a reorientation in investment priorities. A proportionate reduction in investment should be made on a gradual basis to ordinary competitive professions. These professions more readily absorb both domestic and foreign capital and an overconcentration of capital there leads to biased, unreasonable and wasteful allocation of the society's economic resources.

China's state assets should be transferred and concentrated from ordinary competitive professions to its basic industry and non-competitive professions in order to guarantee full development of its infrastructure and enable the full optimization of society's resources. In this way will investment from non-government assets be encouraged. This readjustment is a process that takes time and cannot be accomplished all at once. It should begin from the most urgent and pressing areas of socio-economic life and accelerate from there. Capital drawn from private investment (both domestic and foreign) should be courted and the percentage increased.

In accomplishing optimum usage of "state assets" a new concept of the term is required.

Social benefit vs. economic efficiency   Under the old planned economy system the allocation of state assets was done under a grandiose system involving many different departments and regions, often operating "blind." There was often little return. In other words, huge investments were made but the resulting yield in productivity was low. The net result could be stated to be the wastage or loss of the state asset.

At present, an important reason for the continuing reduction of state assets is that in some areas the management system responsible for these assets is not suited to the transition to a market economy. There is a new concept concerning the utilization of state assets that must be understood to guarantee the full and effective use of these assets under a socialist market economy. The backbone of this concept is the efficient and effective allocation of these assets to guarantee a completely rational and effective system of resources, industrial organization and market structure. Further, a high priority should be placed in utilizing these assets to avoid idleness, minimize waste or loss, reduce production costs, and strengthen management. It is the concept of total overall long-term benefit from these assets that should be fostered. No partial, short-term, individual benefit should be pursued. At the same time any conflict between economic benefit and social benefit must be resolved so as to fully realize proper social benefit while guaranteeing the economic prosperity of the state asset as a primary condition.

The concept of the "value form" of state asset   Readjusting the flow and structure of state asset investment depends to a large degree on the fluidity of these assets—i.e. how convertible. Under the traditional planned economy system state assets mainly took the form of material objects. The state exercised direct control of these objects from raw material to distribution of finished product. In the present stage of readjustment state assets must be called upon to increase the value and liquidity of our currency. For this reason some state assets need to be changed from "form in kind" to "value form." This change does not in the least affect the leading role of state enterprises—on the contrary, it strengthens their power.

New concept of state asset   Will the readjustment of its investment guidelines decrease or otherwise weaken state assets? From an overall and long term view they will only increase. In ordinary competitive professions if non-government owned business is allowed to flow fully, it increases its profits and thus increases the tax revenue. When the national treasury increases, state assets increase also. If this source of income is used to increase investment in new basic industry, it will yield long-term economic benefit as well as increase the total amount of state assets. State assets should be used primarily to develop basic industry, public utilities, and key industry and strategic professions so as to lay down a firm foundation for the entire economy. This greatly accelerates prosperity and development. The utilization of government assets goes hand and hand with socio-economic development. And by strengthening the leading role of state enterprises, the asset base will be greatly broadened.

Concept of competition of state assets   The gradual decrease in the percentage of state assets involved in ordinary competitive professions does not mean competition is not an important factor in operating state enterprises. Under a market economy all sectors must be competitive. In fact, in the spheres related to the economy as a whole and to the standard of living, the wholly government owned enterprises must occupy the leading positions—not to withdraw from competition, but to actively promote it. In the key areas of basic industry and public utilities (where state assets predominate) competition is used to increase efficiency and profits. State assets must compete with non-government sectors and with each other. But in such a way as to not set up barriers between departments and regions. Cooperation and coordination should avoid the wastage and inefficient use of resources that could otherwise result from multiplicity of ownership, duplicative construction, and engaging in blind projects.

C. Bright Ideas for Energizing the State Sector: Fewer New Projects and Better Managed Enterprises

As pillars of the national economy, state enterprises are also the mainstay of the socialist market economy. The practice of over a decade of reform has proven conclusively that where the correct allocation of state assets has occurred, state enterprises have been able to play a leading economic role according to the principles and laws of market economy.

The past decade has also shown some state enterprises lagging behind, stuck between the proverbial rock and the hard place. Unable to advance, unable to retreat. The main reason was the earlier thinking that insisted upon maintaining the huge size of state enterprises at any cost.

It is time for new thinking on the subject of energizing state enterprise. Reform must be aimed at revitalizing the overall economy—not just concentrating on single enterprises.

Theoretically speaking, structuring a new system based on a socialist market economy does not require that the large enterprises formed and operated in the former planned economy era be maintained without change or modification. Realistically it would be impossible for the state to maintain intact every existing state enterprise. The following statistics elucidate this:

—by the end of 1993 China possessed 34.950 trillion yuan in state assets, of which only 74.5 percent were in actual operation.

—the average debt load of state enterprises was 74.3 percent

9

—by the end of 1994 the balance held in deposit accounts by urban and rural residents was 21.5 trillion yuan.

—interest paid on those deposit accounts was 10.98 percent

—annual profit of state owned industrial and commercial enterprises was 7.4 percent

—the rate of inflation in 1994 was over 20 percent

The above facts illustrate the following points:

1) The nominal amount of state assets (estimated at 34.95 trillion yuan) is only 8.982 trillion yuan in real terms after deducting debt.

2) The debt borrowed from banks by state enterprises is estimated at 25.967 trillion yuan (74.3 percent of rate of debt). This is approximately the amount of savings held in deposit accounts by private residents (21.518 trillion yuan). In other words, loans granted to state enterprises by banks comprise 82.87 percent of the deposits of private residents.

3) These residents are actually earning a negative interest from their bank deposits because the profit rate of state enterprises is lower than the rate of interest of the deposits. Maintaining large sized unprofitable state enterprises thus means that residents incur losses. The state inevitably incurs even greater losses. How can such a harmful situation be allowed to persist?

It is perfectly normal under market economy conditions to borrow money to conduct business. But there is a limit to the debt that a business can bear. State enterprises are in debt up to 70 percent of state assets (34.9 trillion yuan). This is excessive and dangerous—ideally such debt should not exceed 50 percent.

The way out is to consult reality—to seek the truth from facts. It is impossible for the state to carry such an enormous debt load. But it will be stuck with this situation as long as it is required to directly run so many enterprises including so many which operate at a loss. The actual amount of state assets is 9 trillion yuan. We must act according to our capability by reducing the size and number of state enterprises and concentrating our financial resources on doing strategic business on a smaller scale and doing it well.

II. Market Orientation of State Assets

A. State Enterprise Makes Transition to State Asset

The backbone of a modern market economy is the energetic and intelligent utilization of capital. To build a socialist market economic system, the central problem is to activate state assets and make them market oriented.

The orientation of a modern market economy is to make profits and to utilize available capital to achieve maximum return. Capital is consolidated and channeled to produce the largest benefits to both immediate profit and to long term capital gains. Around these tasks capital operates.

A socialist market economy is subject to the laws of ordinary market economics. It faces the problems of how to consolidate capital and how to most efficiently utilize such capital to the greatest advantage.

Comprising the largest segment of the capital upon which the Chinese economy is based, state assets obviously exert a decisive impact on that economy. Activating this stupendous amount of capital, conserving and increasing its value, and fully realizing its potential to maximally benefit society—these are the most important challenges under market economy conditions. But only when we have activated state assets can we make them market-oriented. And now, the position of state owned enterprises can no longer be maintained by forceful and artificial means as was possible under a planned economy. No. They can now be obtained only in long term symbiotic relationships with other economic factors. This means co-existing and striving for expansion as a result of fair competition. To succeed in this arena will require state assets to be optimally organized for production, to achieve maximum profits and viability through sound efficient business practices and to make optimum use of its capital. Only when state enterprises keep their competitive edge in the market will they have the capital available to employ in order to control, guide and influence the economy as a whole.

At present, state assets are facing a harsh reality: bigger and bigger losses sustained, devaluation of currency, and the flight of capital. Their growth rate is lower than the growth rate of township and rural enterprises and is lower than that of the country as a whole. Losses have become widespread. Of course this can be blamed on internal causes, but basically it is the entire system of managing state assets which is causing the trouble. Why? Because the fluidity of state assets and the optimum reorganization of state enterprises are restricted artificially making it difficult to achieve optimum utilization and maximum profit. It has also continuously and artificially reduced the value of the asset, such as refusing to transfer the stocks of state assets. Such practices are absolutely not in accord with a developing socialist market economy.

In order to realize the maximum value of state owned assets in a market economy it is necessary to speed up the transition of state assets to state capital and to emphasize the realization of optimum benefit from that capital rather than pushing merely for a greater number of enterprises. That is the basic problem to be tackled in the reform of state enterprises.

From the earlier idea of stressing only the stimulation of state enterprises, we now must move on to emphasize the utilization of state assets and the transformation of existing assets into capital. That is the precondition for successfully establishing a system of modern enterprise in China.

China has been engaged in economic reform for over a decade now. Why is it, then, that stimulating state enterprise is such a difficult problem? The reform has not achieved any noticeable results because it has been following the principle that we must decentralize power and surrender all profit to the enterprise. Attention has been focused on the individual enterprises and on conditions within these enterprises while basic underlying factors stemming from our traditional system are hardly touched. For example, separation of government and enterprise is unresolved—enterprise is still largely under control of administrative departments. The traditional administrative function of government remains basically unchanged. Clearly, with such basic issues remaining unsolved, then such matters as the structure of property rights, optimum organizational form, the mechanics of internal administration, and the cost to be borne by the society will also remain unresolved. So the system of modern enterprise and the exact legal rights of such enterprise cannot be established.

In the first place, the reform of state enterprise is not a problem of individual enterprise itself or of the internal mechanics of an enterprise. Therefore the problems of state enterprise cannot be solved by addressing only the enterprises. The key to the reform of state enterprise is the same key required to reform the entire economic system—making better use of the entire state assets. Only with the full utilization of state assets and the resolution of the administration of state enterprises will it be possible to evolve ideal operating systems so as to achieve maximum production. Therefore the issue of enterprise reform is not an issue of "micro reform." It is very much a "macro reform" involving the reformation of the entire economic system. But to accomplish this we must allow existing state assets to enter the market.

To effect the transition and transformation of state assets into state capital, we must address the overall situation of state assets and not try merely to stimulate individual state enterprise.

State enterprises should foster a reputation for excellence and dispense with any obsolete factors in order to favorably compete in a market economy. The asset and rights of property ownership of state enterprises should enter the market and have the freedom to transfer. Their resources should be reorganized and reallocated so as to achieve efficiency of operation and maximum profits. It is a particularly urgent matter to establish a state holding company which can when needed, in the face of keen competition at home and abroad, provide seed money to strategic projects in state enterprises.

The process from stimulating state enterprise to transforming state assets and from there to utilizing state capital is a great leap forward in the reform of state enterprise. It is also a great leap forward in the transition from the traditional planned economy to a market economy and is the most fundamental issue in establishing a modern enterprise system.

The transition from state asset to state capital does not conflict with the state enterprise's responsibility to discharge its important obligations to society.

Some of the social functions that have been being carried out as a priority by state enterprises can be readjusted as the economy goes through its transition. In principle, the policy of monopoly is abolished. Non-government enterprises should be allowed to operate and compete in suitable spheres. For instance, within certain limits, they can engage in building the country's infrastructure. By policy, all participating units, including state enterprises, should be given comprehensive economic incentives. And appropriate measures should be adopted to deal with the few state enterprises which carry a larger burden of social obligations —calculations can be made and their costs compensated. An earnings index and a profit index should be drawn up and made the basis of an overall performance assessment for rewards and penalties. And in the process of economy progresses, the social obligations performed by state enterprises should be gradually turned over to society.

Under a market economy social functions must be disentangled from state enterprises to allow them to achieve their production quotas and profit goals. Let state and non-government enterprises compete with each other. In this way state enterprises are bound to be stimulated in a positive way.

Contradictions between the material object management of state assets and the "value management" of state assets must be solved so state assets can be put on the market and the transition from asset to state capital can be made.

Under a planned economy state assets were expressed mainly in the form of material objects which were directly allocated and controlled by the government. In a market economy state owned resources get transformed according to the laws of the market. This means that state assets must change from a material form to a more arbitrary form of value. This is carried out according to the principle of exchange of equal value. The government gets back capital as currency of equal value. The state still owns this capital—it does not lose its portion of this capital. But in the process of this change the state actually energizes and strengthens the national economy.

The deep seated conflicts in the traditional state asset management system must be resolved with the utmost zeal to accomplish the transition from state asset to state capital.

Under the planned economy system, the amalgamation of politics with the administration of state enterprise and the handling of capital artificially restrained and handicapped the fluidity of state assets and the evolution of optimum organizational form. This is a deeply rooted factor responsible for much loss and waste of state assets. Therefore the restructuring of the management and operation systems of state assets is key to the successful transition of the economy.

State assets must be placed under centralized ownership and a management system set up. A state asset management committee should be established by the government under which all operational state assets should be placed. Secondly, state assets must be under double-tiered management. The first layer is under the management and coordination of the state asset management (SAM) committee. The second layer carries out specialized management duties. A few professions and industries under state monopoly and control are specifically managed by administrative departments while other professions and industries are under centralized management of state asset management departments. Thirdly, corresponding local SAM committees must be set up in localities. Fourthly, an independent state asset operating system must be formed. This operation will be specifically carried out by the state asset intermediary investment organization (SAIIO). Operation of capital will be separated from business production management of state assets.

B. State Assets Enter Market

Market orientation of state assets implies a complete negation of the former economic system. Under the traditional planned economy state enterprises were under multiple management or controlled by various administrative organs; they were a monopoly and were generally valued in terms of material objects; and they were in a relatively static condition. The traditional management and operation of these assets was done chiefly by direct allocation of resources by the administrative means. Under the old system resources were never allocated through the market. The practice proved that this system had many disadvantages.

The introduction of allocation of resources through market completely negates the old traditional system. When state assets enter the market they accept market adjustments. They operate by and are subject to the laws of the market. Only in this way will optimum resource allocation and maximum economic benefit be brought about.

Another key to the reform of the economic system is the property rights issue. The center of this problem is also the market orientation of state assets.

A central task of the reform of the economic system is the motivation of enterprise. Towards this goal a series of measures have gone into effect since the reform. But the facts show that they didn't do too well. Motivating enterprise is a complicated matter involving many things. The enterprise cannot solve all the above factors by itself. The basic contradiction currently effecting enterprise is property rights. As long as this issue is unsettled it is difficult to motivate enterprise.

Undoubtedly it is necessary to place state assets into the market and to change older operating systems. But this alone is not enough. The problem of enterprise property rights transcends any purely internal enterprise mechanism. The "property rights" issue is based on the observable fact that under market economic conditions the enterprise must be involved with the jurisdiction, definition, allocation, flow, and operation of its property. In fact, it is a problem how the state enterprise will be able to manage and operate itself.

If state enterprises are placed in the market without being freed from the bondage of traditional state asset management and administrative mechanisms, in the end they will have no alternative but to return to the old system. The only way out is to make state assets market oriented as per the above guidelines. This is the basic issue of property rights and a basic demand of a socialist market economy. It is a precondition for the establishment of a strong foundation for a socialist market economy and the basis of overall reform. It is therefore of great significance.

Market orientation of state asset is a pressing and real problem. Reform to China's economic system has made considerable progress. Mandatory planning has been largely abolished. Relaxation of price controls over most commodities has been implemented. But the property rights issue has not been solved and it is impeding further reform.

In the course of our economic reform, experiments have been made in the market orientation of state assets. Stock markets have been set up in some places. Transactions of property rights have appeared in others. Trials on empowered management of state assets and share-holding system have been made. These trials provide adequate preparation and knowledge for the systematic and overall reform of state assets.

We are presently in the process of shifting from an old to a new economic system. A thorough reform of property rights is urgently needed. This is an urgent and real problem and the time for full reform in this area has arrived.

The market orientation of state assets includes the following aspects:

1) Mobility in market: There must be full mobility of state assets in the capital, currency, property, and other markets. State assets will thus operate according to the laws of the market and achieve their optimum value.

2) Maximization of profit: Under the market economy state assets will pursue maximum profits while continuing to increase its value.

3) Independent operation: State assets will operate independently in the market. The government will not directly operate the state assets. Legal person of the enterprise is in charge of the operation of the state assets.

4) Indirect management: State assets will be placed under both unified management as well as decentralized management. But generally speaking management will be done indirectly through a state asset intermediary operation organization. This

guarantees that state assets will be able to operate autonomously in the market without direct interference from administrative sectors.

Characteristics of market orientation of state assets are as follows:

Market orientation of state assets is an inherent demand of a socialist market economy and when such orientation occurs the assets assume characteristics very different from those they manifested under the traditional economic system.

1) Material objects change into value. Under a planned economy state assets took the form of material objects with the government directly controlling their means of production and distribution of products. Under a socialist market economy the value of the assets is determined by the market and measured in terms of price in currency. With the exception of a few state monopolies, the government would no longer exercise direct control over material objects.

2) From static condition to mobility. Under the old system with the government of the direct control, assets assumed a very solidified state unable to flow or circulate. In a socialist market economy state assets must be convertible and able to circulate and operate competitively.

3) Property rights become clear. Under the old system all assets were owned by the state. With a multi-tiered management system, administrative investment channels abounded. The jurisdiction of property rights was unclear and obscure. Under the new system, state assets are held in the form of stocks and operate within the framework of a corporate system. The legal owner of the corporation is given full rights of ownership thus totally clarifying this issue.

4) Deregulation of monopolies. Under the traditional system state assets were operated as monopolies by the state. Under the new system with the exception of a few professions and industries that will continue to be run directly by the state, the assets will be run by intermediate organizations.

5) Integration of administration and enterprise comes to an end. Under the traditional system the ordinary functions of

government were combined with that of ownership and operation of all state assets. Under the new system, government administration will be separated from management of state assets.

Administrative departments in the government have their proper functions which they will continue to exercise. But a socialist market economy requires that administration and assets be separated.

Fresh understanding of socialist public ownership.   Market orientation of state assets requires a change in orientation of its management. No longer will such assets be managed by barter in kind, but instead based on its value as established on the various markets. This in no way changes public ownership, but just redefines it.

1) Under a planned economy public ownership meant public ownership of the means of production, which consisted of physical objects. And means of livelihood belong to individuals following the guidelines of the planned economy. Resources were allocated in accordance with plans drawn up by centralized authority. The old system proved the words of Frederick Engels: Money would become useless—But no longer.

2) Under a socialist market economy the bulk of publicly owned wealth is not in the form of material objects; rather its actual value is measured in terms of currency. And with various forms of ownership (public, private, cooperative) co-existing in a competitive environment, it is now manifestly impossible for the state to control all the means of production. Instead state resources are allocated across the entire economy according to the laws of the market.

3) Changing the country's orientation from material objects (otherwise known as "real assets") to value of objects (known as financial assets) will not at all alter the foundation of socialist public ownership for the change is only effected according to the principle of exchange of equal value. The state will hold negotiable instruments of equal value to the assets it once managed as material objects. There is no loss of asset. On the contrary this capital is now able to be used in other spheres to produce further benefits and a higher asset value. The basis of socialist public

ownership is in no way changed by this—it is only consolidated, developed and expanded.

Fresh understanding of the basic function of socialist ownership. Since under market orientation state assets will circulate and compete with each other, with the profitable being fostered and the obsolete discarded, the question will arise: Does this weaken the basic function of public ownership? The answer to this requires a fresh understanding of the basic function of socialist ownership.

1) Under the traditional economic system public ownership functioned as the overwhelmingly dominant factor in the country's economy. In the words of Frederick Engels, all capital, agriculture, industry, transport and exchange will more and more concentrate into the hands of the state. Non public ownership was considered at best a supplement, occupying a very subordinate position.

2) In a socialist market economy, the basic function of public ownership is to control and operate sectors of the economy relating to overall national viability and standard of living including public utilities and professions and industries that are not well suited to competition. Ordinary professions and industries are developed and managed jointly as public and private ventures which compete on an equal basis in an arena where the efficient will prosper and the obsolete will be discarded.

Under the planned economy system almost all enterprises were publicly owned. But, actually, the true function of public ownership is not in the number but in their combined profit, value and competitive capability. As long as public ownership is taking the leading role in quality, it will be fulfilling its true function. This function can be measured by the success of the national economy.

3) This is in accord with the primary stage of socialism which calls for the co-existence of public, private, and cooperative economic sectors to fully develop the socialist market economy and so enhance socialist productivity. Non public ownership is no longer considered a mere supplement. It is now meant to develop and co-exist with public ownership over a long period of time.

Not, however, so as to occupy a dominant position in the overall economy. But if public ownership continues to be overstressed and everything is concentrated in the hands of the state so as to restrict equal competition among the other economic sectors, there will be an unavoidable weakening of the positive role of the non public ownership sector. This is disadvantageous to the development of the socialist market economy and also out of conformity with the theory of the primary stage of socialism.

Market orientation of state assets is not the same as privatization. This is due to the fact that the fluidity and transfer of state assets and the ease of property transfer on the market are not carried out without compensation to the state. It is exchange of equal value—it is not gratis. Ownership is still retained in the hands of the state, which, therefore, does not lose ownership of the property. The transition from "real assets" to "financial assets" does not change the nature of public ownership under socialist market conditions.

Principles of market orientation of state assets are as follows:

1) Certain professions and industries will continue to exist as state monopolies and will not enter the market. They will be directly operated by the state.

2) By and large the state will maintain a controlling position in state stock companies. According to traditional theory the state should own 51 percent of the stock of an enterprise to guarantee its right to exercise control over that enterprise. But in practice, due to dispersal of stock right, control can be exercised with a much lower percentage of shares.

3) As regards the issue of state assets and the transfer of property rights, due consideration should be given to the continued leading role the state will continue to play in various strategic economic spheres—such are not expected to come under the control of the private sector of the economy.

4) In specific transactions care should be taken to prevent loss of state assets and the mechanics of properly evaluating and supervising such transactions should be strengthened.

Build a state asset market system and orient state assets to the market. There are four kinds of market according to the ways state assets and their ownership is manifested. A stock exchange market, a transfer of stock right market, a property right exchange market, and a transfer of right of management market.

1) Stock exchange market: This kind of market serves state owned stock companies which have issued shares to the public in order to raise loans. These shares are publicly bought and sold in this market. State assets become liquid in the first or second class stock markets.

2) Market for transfer of stock right: This serves companies who have floated bond issues and other limited liability companies. These shares, however, are not sold to the public. If agreement is reached in a stockholders meeting or by Board of Directors, such stock rights can be loaned or transferred. Thus it can flow in the market—mutual shareholding, stock holding, stock owned, and inter-company.

3) Market for exchange of property right: This market serves to transfer or exchange property rights of non shareholding enterprises, including the transfer or exchange at whole or part enterprise, by auction, merger or corporate takeover, marshalling of assets, and intercompany. It could also be used for the exchange or transfer of assets having no stock right in shareholding enterprises such as at bankruptcy auctions, accumulation of idle or surplus assets, etc.

4) Market for transfer of the right of management: This market serves state enterprises controlled, but not directly operated by the state or any state enterprise which doesn't have to adopt the shareholding system. Property rights in such enterprises are not transferred, but the rights to manage such enterprises can be transferred publicly in the form of agreements and contracts. Such transfer or lease of management rights would normally be done through open bidding or competition or through negotiation between intermediary organizations in the market. They must be fixed by contract. Such rights should be ceded to agencies with proven management capability and not to any individual person. Even when granted, such can be re-transferred on the market upon agreement reached by the owner.

Key points in operating a state asset market.

1) The state asset market should be under the authority of the State Asset Management (SAM) Committee and jointly set up and managed by the Ministry of Finance, bank, auditing administration, commission of economy and trade, state planning commission, and state commission for restructuring the economic system.

2) Specific market exchange and management organizations should be set up to each of the four kinds of market mentioned above.

3) A unified national market plus regional markets should be established to stimulate the market system and promote circulation and competition in accordance with differing conditions in different regions.

4) The successful establishment of these markets require their normalization, unification, legal guarantees, open competition, fair dealing, justice and reasonableness.

C. Market Orientation of Management of State Assets

The lag in restructuring the system of macro management of state enterprises is holding up the entire economic reform. Under the traditional planned economy, state enterprises were merely an appendage to the government which directly controlled all aspects of their operation from personnel, finance, and material, to supply, production, and marketing.

If we call the entire nation one "enterprise," then a single state owned company can be likened to a branch factory or workshop of the overall enterprise. In fact, some Japanese experts have suggested that Chinese companies are not genuine companies, but more on the order of a business department or factory of a Japanese corporation. A state enterprise under the traditional planned economy system was just a shadow of a true enterprise, with many of its necessary powers held by other higher administrative echelons and departments. Thus many of its key functions were out of its own control, being run directly by state or government department.

Due to these factors implicit in the older system, the basic problem of enterprise reform does not lay within individual enterprises, but is a broader problem which requires a broader solution. The direction of reform must be from the top down, and not vice versa.

In the fifteen years since economic reform began although there has been some emphasis in separating administration from enterprise management, in changing the role of government over state enterprises, and allowing enterprises to make profit, the overall system remains basically unchanged. Stress is placed on readjusting the relationship between state and enterprise so as to foster greater production but all such reform is going on within the framework of the traditional system. The greatest emphasis is made by casting attention inside individual enterprises so as to change their internal operation. Government departments are supposed to change their viewpoint and give up their power voluntarily. But since the basic system has not been changed, the reform of enterprise continues to fall short of expectation.

Lag in state enterprise reform, then, refers chiefly to lag in reform of the overall system. Only with a new management structure set up in conformity with the demands of a market economy can such matters as property rights reform, restructuring of the internal mechanism of operation, enterprise autonomy, and legal rights, be fully resolved. As long as the basic system remains basically unchanged and continues to follow the traditional framework, reform in these areas is seriously hindered.

If we look at the existing problems facing our state enterprises, we can clearly see that they are being caused by the traditional management system. Some examples of this are government behavior in contractual proceedings, failure to acknowledge the autonomy of an enterprise while its operating conversion is in progress, irregular government behavior in trial shareholding efforts, and difficulties regarding property rights. Simply put, the lag in reforming the overall system has hindered the entire effort of enterprise reform.

Therefore the central problem of state enterprise reform is the failure so far in reforming the overall structure. At present such reform is confronted with many deep layered problems and disagreements. They all involve reformation of the overall system itself. Getting state enterprises on track and productive will not be accomplished before this situation is solved. Due to the importance and key role of state enterprises in the national economy it can be seen that the resolution of this matter is both necessary and urgent.

Ideas on the overall operation of state enterprise.

1) Rebuilding the management structure of state enterprise requires a unified system whose jurisdiction and functions are both fully clarified. Existing state assets are under control of a multiplicity of government departments. Property rights are obscure. A unified organization performing the functions of state asset management on behalf of the state would solve this and so should be set up. A state asset management (SAM) committee could be established in the State Council composed of responsible experienced cadres from appropriate financial management departments plus special state asset management personnel. This will be a centralized management committee in charge of operating state assets and responsible for drafting and implementing needed policy, plans and legal provisions regarding state asset management, operation and supervision. Under this SAM committee a bureau should be set up to take charge of the day to day management work of state enterprises in ordinary economic spheres. Following the establishment of such a committee, government economic management departments will no longer directly manage state assets. This committee will adhere to and demand the separation of administration and assets. Existing government departments which have been hitherto involved in direct control of state enterprise will be merged or streamlined. Executive management functions will be relatively centralized with a double layer management structure—combining centralized and decentralized management. The centralized layer consists of the SAM Committee itself with the overall jurisdiction and power to coordinate and supervise. The second layer will deal with more specialized management. This combination of centralized and decentralized systems will be able to deal effectively with: a) professions and industries under state monopoly and control such as postal communications, railways, banks, weapon-

ry, key mining facilities and public utilities. These are specifically managed by individual management departments of the State Council and would be subject to policy coordination by the SAM Committee. b) Ordinary competitive professions and industries are not suitable for multi government control and management. They should be under unified management of the State Asset Management Bureau under the SAM Committee. Existing departments which have been in charge of ordinary professions will no longer be entitled to exercise direct control over them. They should be made responsible for drawing up policy on professions —later on, semi-official guild association will take over their functions.

This new system should be constructed on a multi-leveled basis of ownership and management. China comprises a large territory. The level of development of its productive forces in the various regions and localities is uneven. Individual provinces and counties have differing and complex conditions. Corresponding local SAM bureaus should be set up under the leadership of local government at the provincial, city and county level. Efficient management will be impossible without the specific address of these different factors by such a multi-tiered management system under the guidance of the senior SAM Committee.

2) Rebuilding the state asset operations system. In line with restructuring the management system, there must also be an independent operations system for state assets. This will occur with the establishment of the state asset investment intermediary organizations (SAII), specifically responsible for the operations of state assets. This is not a management organ, but an economic entity which serves as legal owner of the enterprise in its relations with the market economy. The SAM bureaus and SAII organizations coordinate on an equal basis. The SAM bureaus do not directly operate assets but sends a representative to the Board of Directors or Management Committee of the SAII organization to take part in decision making and supervisory actions. These state asset intermediary organizations consist of investment companies, holding companies, conglomerates, insurance companies, commercial banks, and various types of foundations.

There is a division in structure between the control of state assets and in production operation. SAII organizations are only responsible for the operation of state capital and for investment returns. They do not directly handle business operations. This ensures the special treatment of capital needed to increase viability. Specific business operations are handled by the state enterprises themselves—they are made responsible for production quotas, lowering of costs, raising efficiency and increased profits. And most existing state enterprises would fall under this system.

3) Restructuring the macromanagement system of state enterprises. Under the traditional planned economy every state enterprise was under the jurisdiction of a government department which directly managed it, but management came from many other quarters as well. Under a socialist market economy, this system must be changed. There must be a clear-cut separation between state managerial functions and the operations of enterprise. Government management actions even by legal representatives of the owner (the state) are strictly divorced from the day to day running of the enterprise. Managers of government departments are forbidden to directly interfere with enterprises. They may only provide policy channelling and guidance. The government, through its SAM representative enters into direct dealings only with the SAII organizations in exercising its management and supervisory functions over the state enterprise. It does not have any direct contact or management relationship with those business enterprises which have been subordinated to intermediary organizations. The only command line to the business enterprise is through its SAII organization.

III. Setting Up State Holding Companies Quickly and Trainning State Seed Teams

A. Speed Up Reform of State Enterprise by Setting Up State Holding Companies

Doing so will deepen the reform and is an effective way to

solve many major and important state enterprise problems. Such holding companies (while training groups of state seed teams) can act as a lever that can be useful in promulgating the reform of the state enterprise property right system, restructuring the overall state assets operating system and strengthening internal coordination and internal management.

a) Confronted with fierce market competition state enterprise must exert itself to the limit to catch up in some areas and keep from falling behind in others. State enterprise faces serious challenges in its transition to a market economy. In 1992 nongovernmental industry produced more than 50 percent of the gross value of industrial output (of which collective industry comprised 38.3 percent and individual, private and foreign-investment contributed 13.5 percent). In coastal provinces the figure was between 60-70 percent.

In 1993 the increase in gross industrial output value in Liaoning, an old industrial base, was 11 percent by state enterprises compared to 89 percent by non-state enterprises. State enterprises not only lagged far behind non-government business in that year, but currently are showing an even greater tendency to decline against advances in the private sector.

b) Confronted with this serious challenge in opening up China to the outside world, there is an urgent need for state enterprise to readjust its structure. The vitality of the state sector must be enhanced, specialized division of labor and coordination strengthened and competitive power achieved by means of the formation of state holding companies which can dominate domestic markets while accessing international markets.

Linking up domestic and international markets will impact favorably on many industries and related producers in China. The heavy and chemical and high tech industries which make up one third of the gross value of industrial production and which are almost all state owned will particularly benefit.

Industrial enterprises in China are rather numerous but they are in the main small scale industries, not very productive, but operating at high cost and subsequent low efficiency. China's industry for the most part is much less concentrated than industry in Europe or the USA. This is particularly noticeable in such industries as metallurgy, chemistry, petrochemistry, construction material, power, heavy machine manufacturing, and production of automobiles and electrical appliances. When you add up the total assets of all Chinese aviation companies they fall short of the corporate value of a single US airplane manufacturing company. Take a handful of China's largest producers of iron and steel and their combined assets will not exceed those of a single Japanese steel corporation. Hundreds of Chinese automobile companies have a combined annual output of less than 1.3 million vehicles which is less than the production of a single subsidiary plant of the American Ford Motor Company. Seventy Chinese color TV assembly plants manage to produce 170,000 TV sets per year while the output of only 6 factories in neighboring the Republic of Korea is over 2 million sets for the same period.

As the mainstay of China's national industry, the restructuring of state enterprises is long overdue. Industrial experience in Japan and the Republic of Korea should be consulted. Governmental guidance must be sought to foster and promote amalgamation in certain industries and the establishment of conglomerates to improve China's stature in international markets. Internal management systems are often inadequate while in some groups power has been overcentralized to the point where the autonomy of enterprises is continually violated. It is for these reasons that readjustment of this system must be vigorously promoted. The present difficulties being faced in developing China's companies is due to the remnants of the old system continuing to block progress.

c) Faced with real and serious problems the reform of state enterprise must proceed from an overall perspective. At the end of November 1994 industrial enterprises showed a loss of 41.4 percent, a tendency that was likely to increase. Enterprises are heavily in debt—reported as 71.5 percent but actually closer to 84.1 percent. Many of these debts will be very difficult if not impossible to pay back as state enterprises are burdened by so many social obligations (not to mention redundant personnel). The needed interplay between reform, development and stability can only be accomplished when the state is taking a national perspective.

Setting up state holding companies is one such recommended action. This will accomplish rapid reform of the traditional system and at the same time boost production, improve internal management, and enhance the efficiency and quality of state enterprises.

d) Internal reform of state enterprises in all layers is also called for. Just because we have emphasized the importance of restructuring the overall system does not mean that the internal problems that exist within state enterprises should be ignored or neglected. The introduction of market economy has caused many problems and contradictions within the enterprises. For ten years state enterprises have been made to compete with each other and with non-government enterprises in the market. The state enterprises have been forced to operate at a disadvantage during this time because of the restraints placed on them by the previously outlined vestiges of the traditional system. The establishment of state holding companies is seen to be an important step in reorganization and reform and, under competent management, can go a long way in promoting the SAII operating system and bringing consequent efficiency and increased production to state companies.

SAII organizations take on many forms other than holding companies, such as investment companies, conglomerates, insurance companies, commercial banks and various types of foundations. Some trust companies and investment companies have already been set up. Holding companies are seen as superior in function and one is now in trial operation.

1) A holding company can exercise control over other companies by either direct purchase of shares or buying stock options. This form of control has great flexibility and convenience. Again, the holding company is solely engaged in the handling of assets and does not engage in managing production operations.

2) A holding company carries out state industrial policy. A holding company, by readjusting its investment policy from time to time according to the needs of the state or its own financial

objectives, can promote and strengthen specific professions and industry. At the same time, by making sound financial decisions it does financial control of businesses and provides the state increased assets and facilities with which to steer the overall economy.

3) The unique form of a holding company allows it to form huge conglomerates and extend its tentacles into many spheres. This is done by means of managing its assets. It can even act as a parent company and set up secondary holding companies through which it can conduct more comprehensive business.

4) The prerequisite for establishing state holding companies is transforming state owned businesses to fit into a standard corporate business structure—they must be organized under a share holding system and have independent rights to control and/or dispose of their own property. With fully established stock and property markets in operation the state holding companies will have enough latitude to conduct their business and succeed in their functions—it will also mark the full emergence of the socialist market economy.

B. As an Intermediary Organization, a State Holding Company is an Effective Means to Bring About the Separation of Administration from Enterprise Management

Comparing their performance against international standards we find Chinese state enterprises universally lacking. Serious losses are being incurred and this is chiefly due to the failure to separate administration from business management. With government able to interfere at will and the companies legally restrained from controlling their own finances, state enterprises lack sufficient autonomy to successfully and profitably conduct their affairs.

The introduction of the system of SAII organizations will act as a sort of insulation between the traditional political management structure and enterprise. It will cut any direct links.

a) Specializing in asset management and investment, the state holding company does not interest itself in the running activities of the business who's shares are under its control. The business runs itself.

b) A holding company is a type of independent economic entity brought into being with the development of Chinese company law. It's different in nature from the present professional administrative companies. It is the legal owner of the enterprise.

c) A holding company is also known as a "parent company." A company under the control of a holding company is known as a "subsidiary." By holding (owning) sufficient shares in the company and/or by signing contracts to control other companies, the state holding company exercises actual control over these companies.

d) Both state holding companies and the companies under their control are independent legal entities. Though in a subordinate position, a subsidiary has its own name, sets its own regulations, cares for its own independent assets, assumes external civil responsibilities, and is granted autonomy in production operation. Holding companies must be formed according to company law, so as to guarantee the independent legal status of the state enterprises as well as their right of autonomy of operation. Care should be taken in the formation of holding companies to avoid the errors of the old system—we must guard against allowing the same government departments from continuing to directly manage them under a new guise. Holding companies can be formed through amalgamating already existing state enterprises, by merger, or by purchase of stock.

A key function of state holding companies is the effective build-up of their subsidiaries. If we look at international business practices we will find that small enterprises are generally operated directly by entrepreneurs, not by holding companies. Holding companies generally acquire large and medium sized enterprises which very often already possess needed management and technical skills. The point of a holding company is not to lower efficiency by adding redundant. A holding company can provide help to enterprises under its control in the form of technical and managerial assistance, improved financial practices, promotion, and coordination between different companies without blunting its subsidiaries' own actions or initiative.

a) Holding companies must have as a key duty guaranteeing that state enterprises take a leading role in the market, knowing that such enterprises are really the foundation of a socialist market economy. To accomplish this the independence of both the holding company and the companies it controls must be protected. One of the aims of the holding company is to serve as a buffer against over-enthusiastic interference into enterprise by the government. A state holding company is set up with very specific legal rights and must not be turned into some administrative adjunct of the State Asset Management Committee or any other government department. That same protection must extend to the subordinated enterprises as well. So these require to build a modern enterprise system to guarantee the autonomy of the enterprises.

b) The fluidity of property rights is a cornerstone of a market economy. State holding companies should be established on basis of the fluidity and reformation of state property rights. Holding companies should not be allowed to control all the shares of a company nor take any other actions which would restrict the fluidity of the assets. Stock markets should be established and strengthened, and shares of state enterprise should be listed on those markets so as to be accessible to a multiplicity of channels. This will not only strengthen the value of the companies but will reduce the risk of property loss.

c) Since state holding companies are operating in an arena of competition, they should not take any action which could hinder the mechanics of competition. The state can set up new holding companies or can allow already existing stable and flourishing enterprises to be reorganized into holding companies. But this is all done amidst the framework of competition and no state holding company must be allowed to become a monopoly in a specific business or profession. Exceptions are those specialized areas designated to remain state monopolies. Holding companies should be encouraged to diversify their interests which will both open up previously closed off departments and regions and reduce the chances of them developing into monopolies or seeking to restrict competition in the same market.

State holding companies should be given economic mandates as opposed to administrative or political ones.

a) State holding companies should not be allowed to turn into administrative companies. Recently some professional management departments were reorganized into administrative groups as part of government reform. They continued to use the old organizational management system, followed the old practices and continued to directly manage professions and enterprises. In essence this equates to no change. Care must be taken not to set up "holding companies" which are in actuality just the old government management departments in disguise.

b) With the exception of specific industries or public utilities monopolized by the state, no state holding company should be set up to monopolize an entire industry. Were there to be one holding company for each industry, we would soon see them all turn into monopolies which would seriously hamper competition and is not in keeping with the principles of a socialist market economy.

c) State holding companies must be set up according to economic law and by using economic way. They should not be established by administrative reorganization either by directly forcing a company to become a holding company or by "marrying" one enterprise off to another. It is economic policy which is to be used to guide and protect holding companies. In addition it should be mentioned that holding companies are only one form of state asset management system and that it is not the intention that all state enterprises be reorganized into holding companies or placed under control of one. Simple joint stock corporations should be allowed and encouraged.

C. State Holding Companies Should Be Speedily Established in Keeping with Actual Condition of the State

Currently experiments are underway to set up holding companies in the Chinese aviation, petro-chemical, and nonferrous metals industries. Based on China's real need to effectively utilize its state assets, achieve efficient production, and gain competitive power through inter-department cooperation, holding companies should be set up along the following guidelines:

a) Industries that must be directly controlled by the state such as public utilities, post and telecommunications, aviation, railways, banks, energy, and strategic raw materials should all be operated by holding companies. In these cases the holding companies will exercise control by the acquisition of 100 percent of the stock, by acquiring a controlling interest in the enterprise (less than 100 percent of the stock) or by just entering into a contract.

b) Large scale industries such as iron and steel, automobile and machinery should also be operated by holding companies. These all need to be boosted in terms of efficiency and division of labor and cooperation particularly in specialized fields. Though one of China's central industries, automobile manufacturing is still dispersed, small in scale and weak in international competition. It is particularly urgent for this industry to set up holding companies to meet the increasing international competition.

c) Scientific and high tech industries which require huge expenditures and a pooling of resources for their research should also be run under state holding companies. Such spheres as chemical industry and biological engineering or the electronics industry need the additional help that a holding company can provide to overcome difficulties and solve key problems such as by merger or coordinating resources.

d) China is in urgent need to restructure its economy and streamline its production through improving its technology. An example is China's textile and construction industries which are numerous but small in scale and which operate with out-moded equipment, out-dated technology, and consequently produce substandard products. A restructure of state enterprise so as to form up conglomerates, upgrade industrial production, and enhance labor and management's efficiency is a vital necessity.

e) We must prevent industrial monopolies which have the effect of curbing competition, and by establishing holding companies we in no way mean to encourage such monopolies. An industry like textiles will never achieve optimum efficiency merely by being absorbed by a holding company. But in a system where individual holding companies operate in a variety of areas and produce a diversity of products, efficiency and competitiveness would be fostered.

The formation of state holding companies means that existing state enterprises must be changed to conform to a corporate system.

a) A share-holding system of the state enterprises is the basis for setting up a holding company. This enables the holding company to acquire 50 percent of the stock (or less in the case of dispersed ownership) to permit it to control voice in stockholders meetings. This system also calls for many state enterprises to be formed into limited companies. In handling state businesses organized as sole proprietorships or limited corporations which for one reason or another cannot issue stock, it would only be necessary for a holding company to enter into contract with these companies to place the majority of stock under its control. This is particularly the case in trades and industries requiring monopoly control by the state.

b) Reorganizing state enterprises under a shareholding system is also an effective means of clarifying property rights. The facts of international market have demonstrated that the limited company is by far the most effective and successful form. This has also been found to be true in pilot projects conducted in China. An operating system of limited companies clarifies the subject of property rights, and separates the rights of ownership from the rights of management. As the operation of an enterprise can to some degree be measured by the trend of its stock price and dividends, this system also provides a convenient and objective means of evaluating and improving efficiency.

c) Bold innovations are required to remove artificial restraints on the scope and ratio of shareholding. Through the stockholding system capital can be raised from society to solve fund shortages in state enterprises, technical upgrade projects, and the repayment of old debts. The shareholding system should be expanded to embrace as many enterprises as possible particularly in infrastructure, basic industry and public utilities. It should be extended to include large, medium and small state enterprises. State's monopoly of ordinary shares should be abolished and non-state enterprises should be allowed to buy and sell shares. This will readjust state asset structure as well as go a long way in separating administration from enterprise management. Particular attention should be given to the rights of foreign investors. This is because investors will always weigh potential benefits against the risks involved. Without guaranteed rights to their stocks, foreign businessmen will never dare enter the China stock market. Further, there should be no restrictions on stock ownership and control by foreign investors in non-strategic state enterprises and we must emancipate our minds on this subject.

d) Any double-standard in shareholding must be abolished. Currently on the Chinese stock market the shares owned by the state are not equal in value to those owned by private individuals. But this is not the case with respect to the value of property rights or dividends. This seriously handicaps the healthy development of the stock market and thus the consolidation and increase in value of those shares owned by the state. Any common stocks issued by a limited liability company chartered by the government can be bought or sold on the market by anyone, whether Chinese, foreign, government or private individual. There can be no discrimination and each is entitled to enjoy the same rights as the others according to the number or ration of stock held. Stocks issued must be of equal value, subject to the same risks and responsibilities and liable for the same dividends as well. This will have the effect of raising the value of state owned stocks.

In the interests of more effectively managing state assets while at the same time not crushing the initiative of local regions we must establish both central and local holding companies.

Under a market economy there is a distinction to be made between central and local property rights. Local property rights should be established—this will encourage local government to properly manage public properties and foster efficiency and economy in local state enterprise. In reality such a distinction has already been made in China—there are central state assets and local state assets. Since China is so large a country, and since conditions in different regions are so diverse, it is impossible for the central government to directly control all state assets. Authority must be granted to local government to enjoy property rights. Through the use of tax revenues and the implementation of financial policy the central government will be able to exert control over the economy.

There are two ways to grant property rights to local governments. The first is to place existing local enterprises directly under the jurisdiction of local governments. The other is to deed them a controlling interest in specified enterprises.

State holding companies can only control the property rights owned by the central government while local holding companies control the property rights owned by local governments. In general the need for local holding companies would be less, but such could be useful in public utilities, ordinary competitive industry, and just for increasing economic efficiency amongst enterprises. In such a case the organization would be the same as that operated by the central government. Local SAM committees would also have to be set up to ensure the separation of administration from enterprise management.

IV. Boldly Carrying Out Any Needed Experiments So As to Perfect the Shareholding System in China

A. The Development of a Shareholding System and a Stock Market Will Help in Transforming China's Economy into a Socialist Market Economy

China's march toward a market economy requires the speedy development of a shareholding system. This is vital to building a socialist market economy with Chinese characteristics. The solution to any problems engendered from such development can be found right in the mechanics of market economy.

We are now faced with several problems. Firstly, how can we ensure state assets preserve and increase their value under a market economy? In 1992 there were 68 shareholding enterprises in Hainan, five of which were listed on the stock market in Shenzhen. They registered an annual increase in asset value of

128 percent (not determined by stock price). This shows that the accelerated development of a shareholding system can be an important channel by which to preserve and increase the value of state assets.

And there is a strong demand not only by the state enterprises, but by joint ventures, private enterprises and individual laborers as well, to introduce the shareholding system to enterprise. They see this as a legitimate use of their capital and savings and seek optimum forms of investment.

The shareholding system has played a considerable role in the past two years in attracting foreign and domestic investment, in transforming state enterprise along the lines of a market economy, preserving and increasing the value of state assets, developing strategic projects, and boosting state revenues.

But in the course of accelerating the emergence of this system, problems can be predicted to occur. There will be technical glitches of various sorts and conflicts of policy will surface that will have to be addressed. For example, what should be done with stocks already owned by employees and workers? Allow them to be privatized or not? What about companies who want to enter the market but are forbidden by some policy? The answer is first to solve any contradictions of principle and policy, and then any technical difficulties can be easily resolved.

B. Speedily Allow State Enterprises to Adopt a Shareholding System

The modern market economy's most important form of asset organization is the shareholding system. A corporation is born for the purpose of placing a company into a more advantageous position while engaged in intense market competition. Its most efficient and successful benefit is the concept of "limited liabilities." It was after the emergence of such companies that capitalism entered its peak period. In less than one hundred years it has gone on to produce a productive force greater than all previous productive forces put together. Economists and legal experts in the West subscribe to the view that the invention of the limited company harkened a whole new era and was far more important than the invention of the steam engine or electric power. Without the limited company it would be utterly impossible to harness modern production on a massive scale. The shareholding system has a vitally important role in the reform of state enterprise which cannot be ignored. In fact, the efficient operation of state enterprises is impossible without it. The state assets operation is built with intermediary organizations (such as holding companies and investment companies) as its core. These themselves can adopt the shareholding system by which to invite further capital and they also guarantee the separation of state assets management from its operation.

Implementing the shareholding system accomplishes resolution of the property rights problem in economic reform. It is difficult for big and medium sized enterprises to transfer their overall property rights as part of reform although small enterprises can do so with ease. The most effective solution to this is to restructure the larger companies into shareholding firms to allow adequate fluidity and dispersal of ownership to permit the transfer of assets. To allow for greatest efficiency the state assets should be heavily invested in basic strategic industries and public utilities. State enterprises in ordinary competitive industries should be transferred into shareholding firms to enable the state to pull out from them by selling their stock.

The existing state enterprises will be transformed by different ways. Enterprises operated by government organizations or under direct jurisdiction of government are confined to professions and industries where free competition is deemed inappropriate and so will remain as state monopolies. Enterprises of this type are not market oriented and their assets are non-transferable.

Enterprises are owned by the state but run by someone else. Included in this category are important engineering projects, businesses carrying out strategic plans, large enterprises suffering from heavy losses but which cannot be allowed to declare bankruptcy or be abandoned by the state, and certain other parts of the country's infrastructure. Through trusteeship, contract, or lease, such can be given over to some else's control. The company chosen should have adequate economic power plus a track record to show its ability to straighten out and efficiently run such enterprises. It is not optimum to try and turn small companies into stock companies. Such businesses as small retailing, small industrial enterprises, and service industries (with small capital and employing few people) can be handled better by transferring their assets by means of contract or lease, or trusteeship. They can, when the situation warrants, still adopt a shareholding system or become a privately run enterprise.

State shareholding enterprise: With the exception of the two types mentioned above, the many other large and medium sized state-owned enterprises can all be reorganized into stock corporations. Such can be joint stock companies with limited liabilities or sole proprietorship with limited liability. State shareholding enterprises are the legal owners of the enterprise and have the right to dispose of property, sell fixed assets, dispose of surplus or idle assets, adjust property, hold or transfer shares, buy and sell stock, and even auction or amalgamate the entire enterprise. Corporate ownership does not conflict with state ownership since the state will own controlling interest in the enterprise.

Private operated enterprises: This refers to state enterprises transformed into non-government or civil-operated companies and include medium and small-sized firms plus those sustaining serious losses but which do not play an important role in the national economy. Such firms do not have to be kept as state enterprises and often become more productive when transformed into private companies. Such transformation can be made by stock transfer, amalgamation, or auction.

State enterprises transform into one of three types of corporate structure:

a) Limited liability joint stock company—this is appropriate to the enterprise which needs to raise money from the public to minimize its own risk. Stock of such corporations is placed on the market for trading. Any limited liability company can list its stock on the stock market.

b) Limited liability partnership—it is appropriate for relatively closed enterprises such as joint ventures, cooperative enterprises, or business groups. It takes agreement by a meeting of its

Board of Directors to list its stock on the market.

c) Proprietor sole with limited liabilities—this "one man business" is a special form in the shareholding system. There is only one stockholder and he has limited liabilities. This is an appropriate way to organize enterprises whose stock is wholly owned by the state. It can also be employed by other large and medium state owned enterprises.

Of the three corporate forms, the joint stock company with limited liability is the most convenient, flexible, and efficient structure. It merits our continued attention in the reform of enterprise and wherever it can be applied it should be promoted and instituted.

Specific suggestions in promoting the general reform to the shareholding system.

a) The shareholding system should be vigorously promoted in state enterprises, particularly in industrial enterprises, and no restrictions should be placed on the percentage of state controlled shares.

b) Newly invested projects, projects in construction which show good prospects, key tourism projects, infrastructure projects, as well as other priority projects—all these should be given continuous encouragement and support in the setting up of the shareholding system.

c) Non-government enterprises should also be restructured in accordance with modern principles. Collective enterprises in towns and in the countryside plus private operated science and technical enterprises should be reorganized into shareholding cooperatives or partnerships. The few large scale efficient companies in these categories could also be turned into limited liability joint stock companies.

d) In addition, private and foreign enterprises should be permitted to participate in and promote the reorganization to the shareholding system in order to engender enthusiasm and increase investments. The qualifications of such promoters or sponsors and any restrictions as to their allowed ratio in equity participation should be duly approved and made explicitly clear.

C. Strengthen and Standardize the Management Systems of Shareholding Enterprises

In the course of implementing the shareholding system problems will emerge. Any such should be solved with a standardized management system. Existing problems that have shown up include: lack of specific guidelines in asset assessment and defining ownership rights, confusion as to the actual location of the owner of state assets, failures to guarantee the rights of stock holders, unequal stockholder equity, and unsuitable management systems.

During the reform of the shareholding system, attention should be paid to normalizing the behavior of the government in its roles as promoter and social manager to enable shareholding enterprises to operate at maximum efficiency. The greatest problem that has emerged in the pilot projects has been the lack of exactly set policy which would guide the actions of government. With government behavior unregulated, attempts to introduce the shareholding system can turn into exercises in name only, and not in fact.

Thus legislative work governing the management of shareholding enterprises must be strengthened. Provisional regulations governing the institution and supervision of joint stock companies should be drawn up. A standardized system which incorporates financial setup, personnel handling, labor relations, wages, distribution of profits, utilization of capital, other internal management operations, as well as the function of corporate stockholders, conduct of Board of Directors and Board of Supervisors meetings, legal representation, financial audits, plus other corporate checks and safeguards. The system should include the requirement that joint stock companies must regularly prepare and issue a full report including full financial audit, accounting of assets and liabilities plus full information on profits distribution.

Enterprises organized along these lines are not subject to senior administrative management organs. Existing regulations requiring that management departments approve all operating activities in such companies must be abolished. Any previous arbitrary rules (such as wage limitations) must also be canceled.

It must also be worked out and made clear exactly how the state's rights of asset ownership will be represented.

D. Privately Operated Enterprises Should Also Be Given Support and Guidance in Making the Change to Shareholding Firms

The speedy rise of privately operated enterprise in China has invigorated China's economy. However, this development has its own limitations.

The 14th National Congress of the Communist Party of China in 1992 affirmed the objective of reform to a socialist market economic system. It was made explicitly clear that the guiding policy was to be public ownership as the main force in a long term partnership and cooperation with non-government owned enterprises. From that time onwards China's private sector has been in a state of accelerated development with its previously wavering path left behind. According to estimates by the National Industry and Commerce Bureau there were 184,000 registered private enterprises in China at the end of June 1993, with 2.94 million employees and a capital value of 45.29 billion RMB. This was a respective increase of 87.8 percent, 72.8 percent and 375.7 percent compared with 1990. In the first six months of 1993 the value of the private sector's total product output was 16.15 billion RMB. Business turnover in the same period was 9.69 billion RMB, an increase of 2.33 times and 2.88 times over 1980. Of China's overall industrial output value in 1993 53 percent was from the public sector, while 35 percent came from collective enterprises and the remaining 12 percent from the private sector. Of total retail sales, 40 percent came from state owned commercial enterprises, 30 percent from collectives, and 30 percent from private companies.

This rapid development of China's private sector has spurred the growth of the national economy. In fifteen years of reform the most marked improvements have been seen in the rural and non-state sectors of the economy. In a broad sense, both of these belong to the private sector. Village and township cooperative enterprises have become a new force, popping up almost overnight. In 1992 employees and workers in village and township enterprises in the whole of China amounted to 24.2 percent of the rural labor force, or 17.8 percent of the nation's labor force. The total production of these enterprises was 66.4 percent of the gross rural output and 32.3 percent of the output of the entire country. Tax revenues from this sector amounted to 20.3 percent of the national total. They supplied 42 percent of the total amount of export commodities delivered, and were not only the pillar of the rural economy but the shining stars in middle and small enterprise sector as well.

In striking contrast, at the present time, state enterprises show poor performance and suffer serious losses. That is why the reform of state enterprise has become such a priority. But the development of private enterprises is still in initial stage and is limited by many factors.

a) Most private enterprises, being small in scale, are run as workshops or by the family. These operations play a supplementary role in the overall economy and have difficulty in expanding to a larger scale while maintaining efficiency.

b) They are often utilize crude methods, with many procedures done by hand. This is simple labor with little mechanization or automation. This factor restricts their development.

c) They generally operate with a rather small amount of capital, lacking effective means to raise funds in the society. Thus they have little economic power.

d) Three fourths of these are sole proprietorships or partnerships. Very few are limited liability companies. Even fewer are joint stock companies with limited liability.

e) Most are inadequately managed as family businesses.

Now China's private sector faces pressure from competitors that grows stronger each day. To better operate in such an arena some of these enterprises are spontaneously embarking on the road to becoming a shareholding company.

At a time when state owned enterprises are beginning to adopt reform and likely to shake off their fetters and emerge as a very competitive force, the private sector will lose its superiority if it cannot rid itself of its own limitations.

China is now opening itself up to the outside world in a big way. Foreign businessmen generally regard China as a huge market with very favorable investment conditions. There is strong interest to invest in this country. Meanwhile China is doing its utmost to regain its position in the General Agreement on Tariffs and Trade—now the World Trade Organization. From now on foreign capital and commodities will enter China in great quantities. These will bring additional heavy pressure to bear on China's private sector.

The important task facing the Chinese private sector is to flourish in a modern market economy under all this pressure. Some enterprises, aware of their own limitations and inadequacy, have on their own initiative taken steps to institute the shareholding system, to amalgamate, or to acquire intensive management assistance.

a) The proportion of enterprises adopting limited liability is rising sharply. In 1989 only 4.2 percent of private enterprises had adopted this form. By the end of June 1993 that figure had risen to 22.8 percent.

b) The joint stock company with limited liability has emerged as a key form of enterprise in China. For example the Harbin Dongfang Enterprise Group was approved in 1989 to sell shares of stock in its corporation. Internal stocks issued that year were valued at 36 million RMB. In 1993 the company was approved to sell its shares publicly on the stock exchange initiating a huge buying spree.

c) Private enterprises turning themselves into shareholding cooperatives is a new tendency. In Wenzhou, Zhejiang Province there were 24,000 shareholding cooperatives from 1987 to 1992, whose industrial output value was 48.1 percent of the city's overall total. Tax payments engendered accounted for 45.4 percent of total local tax revenues. Out of 153 shareholding cooperative enterprises under survey, 54 percent were family type enterprises, 36 percent partnerships, 8 percent had cooperative equity participation, while 2 percent were entirely or partly worker-owned.

The cooperative share system is a combination of both the

shareholding and cooperative systems. It is a new type of enterprise system under which property rights are clear, shareholders have direct involvement in the business, and risks are shared by all. Its form is flexible and preferred by many proprietors in this sector because they believe it gives them more stability both politically and economically.

d) Many enterprises in the private sector are entering into joint ventures with public companies. According to a 1993 survey of 143 enterprises with capital exceeding one million RMB, 30 percent had entered into joint relations with state companies and another 23.14 percent intended to form such relationships.

e) Private enterprises are beginning to increase the efficiency and scope of their production. According to survey 40 percent of private enterprises made excellent profits in recent years while another 20 percent achieved definite but less spectacular gains. Thirty percent managed to break even while only 10 percent closed down. Amongst the enterprises making excellent gains the definite tendency was to circulate capital and reinvest earnings. There was also a high rate of accumulation. In Wenzhou, Zhejiang Province, the rate was 56 percent. Many small firms expanded into medium or large scale enterprises. In other regions, the capital of large firms expanded to over 100 million RMB. Big enterprises tended towards amalgamation and cooperative ventures.

Shareholding must be promoted and supported in private enterprise. To adopt themselves to the needs of the modern market economy Chinese private enterprises must expand their own strength and march along the road of the shareholding system. This is needed for the sake of their own survival and development. It is the long term direction for prosperous private enterprises.

To achieve a shareholding-orientation of public or private enterprises requires a number of policy and legal decisions.

By shareholding-orientation we mean publicly or privately operated business which have adopted an organizational structure of a shareholding nature. These include limited companies, joint stock corporations with limited liability, cooperative share enterprises, interlocking equity participation amongst different corporations, merger, plus other systems that assign controlling shares of enterprises by merger or sale or contract.

Private enterprises should be allowed to form up into joint stock companies with limited liability. It was already approved as early as 1988 that such firms could adopt the structure of sole proprietorships, partnerships, or limited liability companies. The development of the cooperative share system should also be encouraged as this system has many benefits and has been spontaneously adopted by peasants—this form of organization needs supplementary legal guarantees to further encourage it. In particular, peasants should be allowed to buy shares with land tenure owing to the fact that land property rights are the subject of continual reform.

Both public and private enterprises should be encouraged to involve themselves in the stock market, buy each other's shares, form joint operations, and when mutually beneficial, to undergo mergers. In particular, public and private enterprises should be permitted to amalgamate with each other. Once the basic organizational forms have been confirmed by law, unnecessary limitations and restrictions which hamper this movement should be abolished. Common fund can be pooled by private enterprises, which may be used to purchase shares of state enterprises. There is no reason private enterprise should not be able to exercise control over ordinary competitive state enterprises through the acquisition of a majority share of stock. State enterprises, other than the relatively few that will continue to be controlled by the state, should be free to choose the form of management that is good for them.

In general it is necessary that the arbitrary restrictions on private enterprises be lifted. Prejudice and unequal treatment of the private sector should just be summarily canceled. The public and private sectors can be likened to the right and left arms of the socialist market economy—as such they must be accorded equal treatment and allowed to fairly compete.

The State Council drew up provisional measures dealing with private enterprises in 1988 as well as complete sets of rules and regulations. However this legislation needs strengthening as obviously some of these rules do not suit present conditions.

V. Accelerating the Reform of the Property Right System

A. The Reform of the Property Rights Is the Decisive Factor on the Overall Situation of Reform

Due to the sweeping implications of the property rights issue and its influence on overall reform, it lies at the root of enterprise reform and must be fully resolved before the development and transformation of enterprise has any hope of going forward.

The 15 years of economic reform in China has progressed through four stages: devolution of power and transfer of profit, contractual management responsibility system, taxation instead of delivery of profits to the state, and the modification of how state-owned enterprises operate.

It cannot be denied that important achievements have been made in the reform of enterprises. However we must also admit that the current level of efficiency of state enterprise is low and losses are serious. At this writing only one third of them are making money. This can be blamed on a variety of reasons, but at the root is the lag in property right reform. Many enterprises have not yet been incorporated, are not operating as independent and autonomous entities, and have no responsibility for their assets. Progress has also been slow in the areas of mergers, bankruptcy declaration, stock transfers, and market transactions. But due to the lag in reforming this area, the full power of state assets cannot be brought into full play.

The accurate summation of the experience of fifteen years has led to this conclusion and just being able to state it clearly shows that an important breakthrough has been made.

Just as it is impossible to have full enterprise development without the resolution of the property rights issue, so is it impossible to have any active market operating. China's market system initially developed from commodities but is currently making the transition to other elements of production. The most important basic issue is still the basis of property rights—without it stocks and shares cannot be traded; assets cannot be transferred. Without these, there cannot be a market. Just as laborers must have the right over their own labor force to produce a labor market, so must enterprises have the rights over their own capital for there to be financial markets.

In the area of rural reform the property rights issue has been raised by villagers. The 1990s has seen the spontaneous development of a cooperative share system (partnership) by peasants who saw it to be to their advantage to cooperate in the production and disposal of certain assets. Of course, this system has property rights as its basis. A problem unique to farming villages is land tenure. Peasants should have the right, after a certain period of land use, to transfer their land tenure. Without such rights, land development will be stalled, and the full power of land resources will never be brought into full play. These factors unsolved greatly hamper general rural development.

The economy is demanding the speedy reform of property rights in its attempts to attract foreign capital. Under modern market economy conditions forms of international investment include direct investment, equity investment, and investment in securities. The last two have been the most popular in drawing foreign investments to China. It has been difficult to attract foreign funds to areas where foreign capital is forbidden equity participation—even in Chinese priority projects. Priority must be given to property rights reform so that China is not denied the full advantages available from the influx of foreign investment capital.

The problem of property rights even looms in the area of social security. Here the issue of gradually setting up personal accounts has been raised. Isn't this just another way to acknowledge the property rights of the individual?

When all these aspects of property rights have been resolved it will then be possible to reform government organizational structure. For the latter depends on two conditions: one, there must be a relatively firm bases in property rights so that no violations are made in places where they should not be made, no allocations permitted where none should be allowed, and no orders given where they are not warranted. There is an unarguable central datum here: property rights. The second condition is market environment. When property rights are finally established as a base a true market environment could exist. Any government actions taken to facilitate this would be appropriate. From whatever angle we look at this issue, the reform of property rights is a crucial issue. It is the foundation of a market economy. So to build a socialist market economy there must be a corresponding property right system.

Of course the market economy in the West is built on private ownership and personal property ownership while a socialist market economy is built on the basis of public ownership. But this also includes the independent right to dispose of property, not necessarily private property. It is an independent right to dispose enterprise property. It allows the possession, use, benefit, and disposal of corporate property according to the law.

Property right is a broad concept encompassing not only corporate property rights but also land tenure (the right to use, operate, and transfer land according to law), and personal property right (legitimate ownership of means of livelihood and production including capital) plus the property rights of communities or groups.

Although major strides have been made in property right reform since opening up to the outside world, the basic issue is still unresolved. It cannot yet be said that an independent property right system exists in China. State enterprises cannot dispose of their property autonomously, peasants cannot autonomously transfer the rights to their lands, and the personal property of citizens (especially means of production and capital) are not explicitly protected under the constitution.

With the advances that have already made, the property rights issue has emerged as the key point of reform which if accomplished would of itself accelerate the full establishment of a socialist market economy.

B. Rebuild the State Enterprise Rewards System with Property Rights at Its Core

A basic contradiction in enterprise reform lies in the mechanism of rewarding production. Under the traditional planned economy the state company is only a cog in the wheel which is implementing policy and programs mandated by the government. It is entirely under the control of the state and receives itself no personal benefits. A major drawback of a planned economy is the lack of vitality of enterprise which directly stems from the inability to reward it for its production. So a basic problem in reforming state enterprise is to solve this problem by the establishment of a genuine rewards system.

The guiding principle of a market economy provides for companies pursuing their own maximum interest through market competition. Since state companies comprise a key sector of the market, they should also, without exception, be provided with their own benefits system.

Some basic relationships are involved in enterprise reform which include: enterprise and promoter, enterprise and government, enterprise and society, one enterprise with another enterprise, enterprise and employees, enterprise and market.

Running through all of these relationships as a basic thread is the existence of the corporation as an independent legal entity. Any problem with this lies in the conflict of interest between the corporation's current market goals versus its other responsibilities brought forward from the days of the traditional system.

The key to the success of enterprise reform is the success in reform at all echelons and regions, whether micro or macro—that and the establishment of a genuine enterprise rewards system. The best criteria by which to judge the effectiveness of the overall reform is to observe whether a real rewards system has been established for state enterprise.

A rewards system for state enterprise involves three basic areas of potential conflict:

a) Between the enterprise and the state. The "interest relation" between enterprise and state may be described as two-tiered.

The first is the interest relationship between the state as promoter of the state enterprise and the enterprise. The second is the relation between the state as the manager of the economy and the enterprise. Under the traditional system these two statuses were mixed and the functions unclear—this led to conflict of interest between the state and enterprise and continues to act as a block to the reform of the system.

When an original property owner invests property in enterprise, it should enjoy stock rights and independent property rights as the legal owner of the enterprise. This is its due. In practice, however, the owner of the enterprise does not possess such rights and still comes under arbitrary state interference.

As promoter of enterprises, the state should have the same interest as the enterprise. The state should stress the long term development of the enterprise and encourage conditions which permit maximum growth. But in practice the state withdraws most of the profits from enterprise often creating a serious shortage of capital flow. This makes it very hard for the enterprise to effect needed changes and causes poor prospects for future development. Further, the state not only interferes with the autonomy of the enterprise but heaps a heavy social burden on it, requiring it to make contributions and allocating its money to various purposes from time to time.

b) Inter-relationship between the enterprise and its employees

There are three questions involved in this relationship: 1) To what if any extent should employees enjoy labor force property rights derived from the wealth they have created for the enterprise (in addition to wages and bonuses); 2) To what if any degree should employees take part in decision making in the operation of the enterprise and in the disposition of its assets; and 3) To what if any extent should enterprise assume responsibility for employee social welfare, social insurance and the disposition of redundant personnel.

Under the traditional system employees do not benefit from the wealth they have created for their enterprise nor do they participate in decision making concerning the enterprise's operations. On the other hand, the social burden of the employees is shouldered entirely by their enterprise. These dynamics can conflict when the workers wish to obtain increased benefits while the enterprise becomes unwilling to continue to assume a burden it claims actually belongs to society. The relationship between these two forces needs to be refashioned.

c) Interest relation between enterprise and management

Under the traditional system there was no independent business management of state enterprises. The factory director or manager was regarded as, and was in fact, an administrative official. Under market economy, management must grow into an independent force. Factory directors and managers can no longer be regarded as administrative officials. They must apply for a job but it will be their skill, experience, and previous results which will determine if they are employed. This will inevitably result in the formation of an independent managerial and entrepreneurial class. The relationship between this class and the company will be based on some sort of rewards and penalties system—and the rewards or penalties received will be closely linked to the efficiency and production of the enterprise being managed. A question that will need to be resolved is to what extent if any that such a managerial class will be permitted to enjoy the property rights of the wealth it has directly created for the enterprise by its skill and effort. In a modern market economy management is a form of capital. A skilled effective manager can be worth his weight in gold. How a socialist market economy can manage this capital is a question that will have to be conscientiously confronted and answered.

The idea of a reformed system of property rights, as described above, may come as a new concept to many and may go deeply against some long held beliefs. If so we must emancipate our minds and change those concepts for this issue is one of the most crucial we face in the transformation of our economy.

Another new concept is the corporate system. As we implement this system we must keep in mind its basic difference from our traditional system. It is based on the concept of private responsibility of property. It is not set up on the basis of public ownership and government administrative control.

A third new concept is state capital. The old concept of state owned enterprise must be thoroughly transformed through the concept of state capital. This will required new forms of management, investment and organization form and operation. (Of course the state sole proprietorship in certain individual monopolized industries will not be abolished.) A new path must be pursued with diversified investments of state capital becoming the vehicle by which to preserve and increase the value of state assets.

C. The Share Economy

For the past two years China's share economy has made rapid progress and exerted an important impact on the socioeconomic life of the country. But it is still in its initial stage, immature and fraught with contradictions. Nevertheless, preliminary results fully confirm that the share economy has greatly promoted the integration of enterprise into the market system plus accelerated the overall growth of the national economy.

In the traditional system the state owned everything including bath houses, barber shops and small restaurants. This factor alone prevented the state from playing a full role in modernizing and developing the national economy. We must now emphasize efficiency—efficiency of basic industry in the development of the national economy, efficiency in management, and efficiency in the service industries including public utilities. Grasping this concept of efficiency will make it much easier for us to solve the problems of property rights in state owned enterprise.

Convert a creditor's right into stock: the role of stock right in a share economy.

In the course of history state enterprise has amassed an enormous quantity of debt. Many reasons have been attributed to this, but irregardless, the dissolution of this debt is a key issue in enterprise reform. In productive companies with efficient marketing and excellent business prospects, these debts to banks and non-financial institutions should be converted into shares to lighten the burden. This will go a long way towards freeing debt ridden enterprise from their indebtedness. It will also promote the transformation of special commercial banks as well as speed up the reform of other financial institution.

Peasants land use rights: a specific form of property right and its role in the share economy.

It has become popular to recognize and protect the property rights of peasants in the form of land use rights. This inspires the enthusiasm of peasants to develop their land.

City development is now increasingly and intimately linked to the development of the suburbs, particularly in coastal areas. It has been proven that the combination of capital, technique, and rural land has greatly promoted the development of rural areas. Peasants are trained and allowed to become employees of a company. Then, they are allowed to legitimately transfer their land use rights thus developing the share cooperative economy in the countryside.

D. Property Rights of the Labor Force in the Reform of State Enterprise

When we talk about reforming state enterprise in China what we are really talking about is maximizing efficiency and profits. The two chief conditions necessary to reach this goal are the correct allocation of resources and the prudent distribution of profits. Although important strides have been made in certain areas, no real breakthrough has been made in enterprise efficiency and profits. Experience clearly tells us that to achieve the required efficiency the first thing we must do is reform the property rights system in a way that is compatible with Chinese conditions. In the absence of such a system it is senseless to speak about a market economy. Some enterprises have employed outside managers under contract to improve efficiency but this is neither a universal nor long term solution. Reforming property rights will go a long way towards increasing efficiency of state enterprises by permitting the most advantageous allocation of resources. Such reform involves three distinct sectors: the property rights of public shareholders, the property rights of the enterprise itself, and the property rights of its labor force. It is possible that we may yet achieve the goal set forth by Karl Marx whereby the laborer, while continuing to do his labor, at the same time becomes a part owner of his company. This means that in addition to his wage and any bonus, he would also enjoy to some extent the benefits of the wealth he has helped the company produce. This would be done by transferring a percentage of the profits of the enterprise over to the employees in the form of dividend producing stock. (The amount to be based on such factors as working hours, post responsibility, and the actual production of the individual employee.) Stock so obtained may not be transferred, exchanged or inherited. Implementing this system rewards the value of labor.

The interests of enterprise and labor may not always be seen as the same, but any reform of enterprise must include the rational coordination of the two so as to promote a long term stable development of state enterprise in the environment of a market economy. Existing conflicts include:

a) Conflict of interest between the laborer on the one hand and the enterprise and state on the other. Under traditional planned economy the state enforced a highly concentrated labor wage management system by which one employee received the same treatment as any other regardless of his production in the enterprise or the enterprise's overall production. The allocation of production factors (including labor) was based on political or administrative motives—not on production.

Under market economy conditions the urges to achieve the optimum utilization of state assets, the maximum profit by enterprise, and the most benefits possible by labor are all inevitable. As the system giving "equal treatment to all workers" breaks down, the better workers will flow into the jobs requiring increased responsibility. The reward and penalty system for workers will persuade them that the best interest of the enterprise is also tied into their own best interests. And with the flourishing and prospering of enterprise, the state assets will also flourish. Any conflicts between these forces must be studied and solved. This is not giving away state assets to individuals, nor is it privatization. It is a correct handling of the potential contradiction between the three forces listed above in a way that will expand and stabilize the earnings of state assets and guarantee the government's long term interests.

b) Conflict between short and long term interests. The sometimes irrational behavior of enterprise can often be traced back to an attempt by laborer or manager to pursue its own short term interests. In the initial stages of transition from a planned to a market economy it is unavoidable for the laborer to seek maximum short term interests for himself. Enterprise, on the other hand, can resort to temporary wage hikes as a short term measure. The excessive pursuit of short term interests by either enterprise or laborer can jeopardize the long term interests of both. Granting workers increased property rights in the form of stocks can solve the contradiction between personal income and corporate profits rather well. As the more profitable the enterprise the higher the dividends the workers will receive, they will soon discover that it is in their own best interests to increase their consciousness and participation in the management of the enterprise. The enterprise and worker will share a common fate and the recognition of this bond will solve many of the apparent short and long term conflicts.

c) For a very long time we recognized the fact that increased efficiency stemmed from optimum investment of capital and but gave no importance whatsoever to the role of labor. For one thing, weren't the returns far greater when capital was invested into material resources rather than labor? This was the opinion, but an opinion which led to laborer pursuing all kinds of short term opportunities and means to increase its own personal financial gains. By integrating both human and material resources as capital, the various elements can be combined so as to enhance labor productivity.

The quality of management and its spirit of responsibility are important elements influencing the efficiency and performance of enterprise. The role of management becomes even more important following the introduction of the property rights system in the enterprise. The emphasis on human resources very particularly includes the role of the enterprise manager in the development of his company. Solving any contradictions between labor and enterprise are important to the development and reform of enterprise—and it is totally possible for them to be solved.

The plan to publicly issue stocks to employees and workers was first proposed by Louis Keleso, a noted American lawyer, in the early 1960s. His idea was to allow employees a credit account on the company books essentially giving them ownership of capital. Later the employees could use income from this capital ownership to pay back these credit accounts. Following suit, many other Western countries widely adopted this system. Right now there are many companies which proclaim themselves as having stocks owned by employees. In the course of denationalization in Britain over 90 percent of non-state-owned companies have implemented this system. In Japan by 1990 out of 2,710 companies listed on the stock exchange, 1943 had stocks owned by employees. In 1975 a public opinion poll showed 66 percent of people in the U.S.A. were in favor of employees owning a majority of company stock. Another poll in 1978 showed 64 percent of employees in the USA thought that if all employees and workers were allowed to have an equal share in company dividends the productivity of labor would rise. Implementing this system is an important measure in harmonizing the various interests during the transition from planned to socialist market economy. It will also help sustain economic growth and stabilize the society. Rewarding workers will inspire their enthusiasm and consequently raise the efficiency and performance of enterprise to the highest degree. Of course placing a priority on efficiency does not mean we forget justice. Of course certain restraints will need to be laid down—provisions for an "upper limit" in property rights are needed to avoid new contradictions.

In a period of accelerated reform of state enterprise we must take the lessons learned in selected experiments and carry them over into wider areas. The benefits experienced by enterprises which have adopted property rights for labor have encouraged many others to follow suit. In large state companies that have adopted this system, the ratio and amount of property rights allocated to laborer has been successfully determined by negotiation. Smaller state owned operations have successfully converted into civil-run but state-owned enterprises so that laborer could attain a larger proportion of property rights. Those state owned enterprises suffering serious losses should enlarge the proportion of property rights to its labor force and gradually establish a fund to offset social benefits. This will ultimately solve at least part of the source of its serious losses. Enterprises which were originally collectively owned have formed a more direct and extensive form of social benefits fund and through the granting of property rights to the workers became actual "worker-owned" enterprises.

We suggest that certain enterprises be chosen as sites to experiment in the area of labor property rights. A sustainable interest distribution relationship can be built between enterprise and employee to build a mechanism that will stimulate labor to greater production. Many forms can be adopted to experiment with these property rights such as collective trust stock, personal account stock, employee share associations, etc. Trust foundations or employee share associations are perhaps more stable forms that should be adopted at first, but in any experiment, the following must be taken into consideration:

a) Equal distribution of shares will not inspire employees to work hard and will not make up for earlier losses sustained by the enterprise.

b) Short term behavior should not be taken in such a way as to make it impossible to change later. For instance, limiting the scope of laborer's property right, leaving no room for maneuver, should not be done. The percentage of laborer's property right in an enterprise is relatively stable, but the yield from that capital will vary and the relative amount going to each employee must be readjusted every year according to post, production, working hours, etc.

This system can and should be implemented in non-state enterprises since it involves the vital interest of the broad mass of workers.

But the sequence that should be taken is to first carry out experimentation in chosen areas to gather experience. Then gradually implement it over a wider area. Such things as rushing in headlong with mass unproven actions should be avoided. To ensure smooth implementation, government leadership at various levels must be strengthened and then make decisions based on experience gained from experimentation.

The close integration of the mutual interests of enterprise and employees is an important precondition for the success of a modern market economy. We can and must solve any contradictions between these two interests so that a permanent and expanding power is injected into the socialist market economy achieving the ultimate goal of common prosperity.

Implementing a system of property rights for the labor force is therefore an important cornerstone in the reform of state enterprise and in the establishment of an ideal socialist market economy.

Chapter II
Macroeconomic Reform in the Changing Trend of China's Economy

China must accelerate her macroeconomic* reform as she makes the transition to a socialist market economy. If we don't dispense with the national economic routines in use under the traditional planned economy we will never be able to fully establish a market economy.

Although a market economy does require macroeconomic adjustment and control, such must be based on a market economy pattern—a very far cry from the old ways.

In the first place we must demarcate lines of jurisdiction between central and local authorities. And in the second, any macroeconomic adjustment must have as a basic goal, the curbing of inflation. The test of any adjustment or control steps is whether reform can be accomplished while maintaining sustained high speed economic growth. The accomplishing of all these points requires the following factors to be studied and resolved:

---

* "Macroeconomics: the study of the economic system as a whole especially with reference to the general level of output and income and the interrelations among sectors of the economy—opposed to microeconomics."

"Microeconomics: a study of economics in terms of individual areas of activity (as a firm, household, prices)—opposed to macroeconomics"

—Websters Third New International Dictionary (unabriged)

I. Macroeconomic Reform in the Transition to a Market Economy

A. China's Macroeconomic Reform: History and Main Issues

Since the end of 1978 China has been travelling the path of economic reform, attracting worldwide attention while doing so. The GNP increased by an average of 9 percent per year. The power of the traditional planned economy declined sharply in the face of continuous advances by the market system. By 1992 China had publicly announced her goal to establish a socialist market economy symbolizing the start of an important new phase of development.

Prior to 1978 China's economic system was a highly centralized planned economy. The government not only controlled the gross national product but also directly managed all the important individual production activities. The country's revenues and expenditures were all controlled by central government. The state also directly controlled allocation of resources in according with national strategic plans and priorities. Allocation of finances was similarly determined. Government had direct jurisdiction over all enterprise and management was just the means of executing government policy.

As macroeconomic reform began to crystallize following the devolution of power from government to enterprise, the market began to develop as enterprise gained increased autonomy.

Since '78, the reform of the Chinese economic system has gone through three stages:

First stage: December 1978 to October 1984

At the end of 1978 the Third Plenary Session of the Eleventh National Congress of the Communist Party of China focused the work on economic construction. The Central Committee clearly marked the restructuring of the national economy as its historic mission. It is this which preceded China's structural reform.

During this stage the main problems to be solved were overconcentration of power in management, failing to separate the functions of government from those of enterprise, equal treatment of enterprise and labor irregardless of production. Reform must go in a direction that curbs the state's power over enterprises and allows those enterprises to retain a greater share of the profits it produces.

This structural reform actually began in the countryside and consisted of three aspects:

a) A contracted responsibility system replaced the highly concentrated "peoples communes." Lands were placed under contract to farming households to be managed by them on an individual basis. Land tenure, however, still belonged to the collective.

b) Next came price reform. Price supports for farm produce and ancillary products were enacted and a purchase order system was adopted. Distribution lines were opened up and adjusted by market forces.

c) Further reform sparked the emergence of village and township enterprises which soon became the most important elements in the rural economy.

While this rural reform was moving ahead other experiments were on going to expand state enterprise autonomy over production activities, central cities were for the first time allowed to play their part in the economy, Special Economic Zones were being established, coastal regions were encouraged to woo international investment and in general the country was being opened up to the outside world.

Various changes in management occurred that gave increased autonomy to state companies including a measure of determination over their own finances. State owned enterprises no longer had to hand over all their profits to the central government. Taxes were substituted for "profit delivery." From that evolved the first rudimentary tax structure. After 1979 special banks were re-chartered or newly set up. Also a Central Bank was established. Mandatory agricultural plans and programs were reduced to a point where they'd been all abolished by 1985. Even the State Planning Commission's centralized distribution and allocation systems were being dismantled.

Second stage: October 1984-1992

In October 1984 the Third Plenary Session of the 12th National Congress of the Communist Party of China announced a decision to reform the country's economic structure which would send it in the direction of a market economy. In 1987 the reform moved ahead even further with the adoption of the principle that the state would regulate the market and the market would guide enterprise. At that time enterprises were granted even greater autonomy (including making them responsible for their own profits and losses), a healthy market environment was being fostered, and government started using indirect methods to control enterprises in place of directly interfering with their operations.

Urban reform was the priority during this stage. Emphasis was placed on strengthening the vitality of state enterprises. Reforms were undertaken in the fields of management, planning, investment, finance, taxation, pricing, banking, materials, commerce and foreign trade. During that time we also saw gradual cut backs in both central planning and in government price fixing.

Tax rates were adjusted. At the end of the 1980s and beginning of the 90s experiments to separate taxes and profits were conducted. The banking system also underwent a series of reforms including the speedy development of money and capital markets. New (indirect) means of adjusting the economy were employed and economic control was strengthened through the judicious use of interest rate, tax and exchange rate.

Third stage: 1992 to the present

In October 1992 the 14th National Congress of the Communist Party of China made clear its objective of setting up a socialist market economy. It affirmed the position of the market and its basic role in the allocation of resources (under state macro-adjustment and control). The plan was to guide the traditional planned economy through a planned commodity economy stage to finally emerge as a full socialist market economy.

The Chinese government made rather great efforts in macro adjustment and control in the summer of 1993. Fluctuations and an overheating in the economy called to attention to the fact that acceleration was required in the reform of economic structure. 1994 saw the adoption of a further series of reform measures in the areas of finance, taxation, banking, investment, foreign exchange and trade, as well as the management and organization of state assets. The objective was to establish a basic framework to permit state macro adjustment and control under the socialist market economic system.

Some of the macro economic measures that were adopted met with rather good results, but it was recognized that under the system as it existed, such measures could only be of limited value.

The main problems in the economy at the time included:

a) An unfair system of taxation. This chiefly manifested itself in a tax base which was too small and depended too heavily on tax revenues obtained from processing industry and state owned enterprise. Changes in the economy led to unstable tax revenues. There were too many inequities carried over from the planned economy—fixed price—days. Some adjustment had been made, to be sure, but overall taxation policy remained exceedingly slanted. There were too many tax items, too many tax categories, and varying tax rates given to different forms of corporate structure. This destroyed the uniformity and standardization of the tax system opening the door to various forms of tax evasion and making it very difficult to either collect or manage taxes.

b) Under the then existing system, local governments were responsible for their own finances. But as structured, this system was inadequate to handle the relations between state and local authorities. Government authorities could not be pried loose from direct control of state enterprise. Local turnover tax was too high which impacted heavily on the economic structure with companies frantically (an inefficiently) trying to expand their activities. The central government's financial resources became insufficient and macro financial controls were weakened.

c) The functions of financial institutions were not clearly delineated. The Central Bank had the job of fostering economic growth while also being responsible for currency stabilization. At the same time it was swamped with too many obligations associated with economic structural adjustment. With insufficient financial tools at its disposal, it came to rely almost exclusively on controlling the volume of currency as the means to accomplish its aims. This conflicted with the law of supply and demand—currency outside the orbit of state planning could not be brought under control while priority construction projects within the realm of state planning were jeopardized.

d) Although direct economic interference by the state had diminished, no substitute form had found by which the government could exert its power in the market economy. There was no coordination between planning, finance and banking.

e) Investment policy was overcentralized in the hands of government departments. This manifested in a lack of coordination in fund raising and construction in addition to dispersed decision making on investment priorities and debt repayment schedules.

As price controls were relaxed and business activities accelerated towards market orientation, conflicts in the existing business system intensified (administrative management vs. market). The deepening of macro-economic reform became an urgent priority in guaranteeing stable economic growth.

B. Basic Format of the New State Macro Adjustment and Control System

The main objectives of state macro adjustment and control are as follows: to maintain a basic equilibrium of economic forces, promote economic stability and growth, handle any deficiencies in the market mechanism, provide public goods and services to society, adjust distribution of income, maintain social equity, promote the balanced development of regions, adopt suitable industrial policies, and promote business reorganization in order to raise the capacity for increased production.

The general format is as follows: Monetary policy is the primary tool used to adjust and control overall supply and demand. Financial actions are taken to adjust economic structure. Industrial policy plays a functional role in forwarding state priorities. The function of planning is to outline the sequence of targets to forward the prosperity of the national economy and also social development.

More specific elements to the reform include:

1) The main function of taxation is to provide a stable income base for the government and to create circumstances that allow for equal market competition. The tax policy has been evolving as part of a transition that was postulated to end in the neutralization of taxation.

To this end the tax system has undergone a lot of reform. A standard value added tax was introduced and replaced earlier unfair corporate taxes. Consumer taxes were levied on certain special consumer goods where the tax burden had been considerably lightened by these changes. A unified corporate income tax and individual income tax went into effect. Prejudicial regulations (that slanted tax rates depending on the form of business ownership) were abolished.

Individual income tax rates on Chinese and foreign nationals were standardized. The scope of taxes levied on property and other resources was expanded to promote the effective use of those resources. Value added tax was applied to all housing and real estate transactions. And a progressive income tax was assessed on those who realized particularly large profits from their transactions.

2) Through the redistribution of revenue returns and utilization of state capital, the financial system is meant to be able to provide infrastructure facilities and social services to the public, promote the balanced development of regions, and maintain long term stable economic growth. At the same time monetary policy is used to adjust the overall level of supply and demand. To fulfill those functions a financial system was implemented with tax returns shared by central and local governments.

According to existing demarcation and division the central government's finance is used to cover the government's operating costs including expenses to do with national security, foreign affairs and other causes directly managed by the central government. Local government pays expenses related to operating local government, economy and institutions.

Those taxes which go towards the maintenance of central

government activities are called central taxes. Those which are intimately related to local economy and social development are called local taxes. Certain other taxes are fixed as joint central and local government taxes to be divided according to prevailing conditions. Separate taxation bureaus exist to administrate these two types of revenues.

3) A central bank "macro adjustment and control system" was set up to enable the state to independently implement monetary policy under the leadership of the State Council. A number of financial organizations were set up, with state commercial banks playing the leading role. Orderly competition is promoted but under strict control. Making the central bank into a genuine central bank was recognized as key to strengthening financial reform. The functions of the People's Bank of China were laid out as follows: to draw up and enforce monetary policy, to maintain stable currency, to strictly enforce supervision over financial organizations, and to regulate the safe and effective operation of the country's financial system.

The central bank's monetary policy is a very important means of macro adjustment and control. Financial policy's short and medium range goals include maintaining the volume and supply of currency, regulating the total volume of credit and setting the interest rates and limits of interbank loans. The long term goals, of course, are to maintain a stable currency and promote economic growth. The central bank must supervise the banking industry and maintain financial order. However, it does not interfere with the business of specialized banks.

There was a distinction made between banks which carried out government policy in economic spheres and banks that conducted purely commercial business and both kinds were set up. The former was backed entirely by state credit, attracted long term capital investments, and were used to fund infrastructure and basic industrial construction projects. Such banks operate autonomously, assuming their own risks, but always under the guidance of state industrial policy and planning. They are not motivated by the goals of commercial finance—their goal is to preserve and increase capital with small profits. These "policy banks" consist of the State Development Bank, Import-Export Credit Bank, and Agricultural Development Bank of China.

The existing state specialized banks—the National Industrial and Commercial Bank of China, the Agricultural Bank of China, Bank of China, and People's Construction Bank of China are being reorganized into genuine commercial banks, operating in accordance with modern commercial banking procedures. Other national and regional banks are also being reorganized into commercial banks.

At the same time cooperative banks are being set up in the countryside, developing out of the urban and rural credit cooperatives. These cooperative banks undertake commercial banking business, chiefly serving medium and small enterprises, agriculture and economy of developing regions.

A financial market is being developed and continuously strengthened—banks float bond issues. Standard banks provide interbank loans. A better relation needs to be worked out between the interest rates given on straight loans as compared to bonds and other marketable securities that reflects differences in maturation periods, cost and risks. Margin limits must be enforced to reflect a rational relationship between market supply and demand. Bond market should be further developed and perfected. More public stocks will be listed. The second class securities market will be further expanded. Mutual funds will also be developed. Small and medium investors will be encouraged to participate in securities investment to spread and reduce the risks in investment.

4) Foreign trade and foreign exchange must be further reformed to step up the opening up of China to the outside world. Autonomy must be granted in the running of foreign trade organizations. Conglomerates oriented towards foreign trade should be developed. Macro control of foreign trade should be explored and perfected. Import regulations need further reform. Inspections and regulations by government should be in the main reduced. The role of chambers of commerce should be strengthened. Licensed public bidding and auctions should be set up. A comprehensive set of laws and regulations on foreign trade need

to be set and made well known.

The foreign exchange control system has already undergone change. Policy on foreign exchange must be coordinated with monetary policy. The long term objective in the reform of foreign exchange control was to make the Chinese currency Renmenbi directly convertible into foreign currency. In 1994 the former "double exchange rate" was abolished, and a single rate was adopted which fluctuated on the basis of market forces. (This exchange rate was still subject to control.)

Other changes included the abolition of the so-called "foreign exchange retention quota" which was replaced by straight settlement. The system requiring planned examinations and approvals of regular foreign exchange payments from current accounts into international trade projects, labor cooporation and activities introducing foreign technology into China was also abolished. Permission was granted, under certain circumstances, to convert RMB into foreign currency in current accounts. The "Foreign Exchange Adjustment Center" was replaced by a national interbank foreign exchange market. At the same time strict regulations were put into effect forbidding unauthorized foreign exchange quotations and circulation of foreign currency.

Opportunities must be seized to further open up China to the outside world. More regions and territories must be opened including those along coasts and rivers, in perimeter areas, and those following trunk communication lines. Service industries must also be expanded. An extensive program needs to be pursued to attract foreign investment capital (including securities investments).

5) The chief function of a planned economy system is to study and work towards long term strategic goals, to develop medium and long range plans and programs and industrial policies that forward those goals, and to ensure that all such economic development is done with due regard to the stability of the economy as a whole.

Under market conditions, however, all state plans and actions must be of a guiding nature and consult the market. Priority should be on medium and long term plans. Annual plans should be simplified and targets reduced. Those that are retained should be modified and aligned to the overall strategic plans.

In addition, the investment system must undergo further reform. Enterprises must be given the autonomy to make their own investments, and be held accountable for those investments.

6) While all the above are going on the social security system must be strengthened. A multi-level social security program must be established which includes social insurance, social relief, medical care, social welfare, and special benefits for the dependents of those who die in work related accidents. This should be a combination of state assistance, individual health insurance plans, and contributions from enterprise. The idea is that once the pension scheme and unemployment insurance are fully established, the burden on enterprise should diminish. Commercial insurance companies could be utilized to supplement social insurance.

II. Reform of the Macroeconomy Must Fully Utilize the Initiative of Both Central and Local Sectors

The initiative of both the national and local economic sectors must be brought into full play. The aim is for more localities to develop fully under the guidance of the macro control and so speed the growth of the national economy. Such a plan has historical precedent in China.

A system whereby tax revenues are now shared by central and local governments now exists in China. This is similar to systems that have been universally adopted in countries with market economies. Its introduction into China is advantageous in standardizing the economic relationship between the central and local governments. But those administering this system must free themselves from the old paths of over-centralization which dampen the zeal of local departments. Stress should be placed on separating economic functions from political ones.

But in implementing any such system, the actual condition

of China must be considered.

a) China is a big country and the development of its socio-economy is uneven. The economic base, natural conditions, culture and geography vary greatly from region to region. It is impossible to have identical levels of economic development in all regions.

b) Places with more favorable conditions obviously forge ahead faster, but it must not be forgotten that this accelerates not only their own regional economic development, but stimulates the progress of other areas as well. An example is the development of coastal regions which clearly promoted further inland development and hastened the development of the entire economy of China.

c) The central government can no longer take broad sweeping national actions such as earlier under the planned economy. Since the development and productive forces of different regions are so uneven, allowances must be made and local authorities must be given the autonomy and flexibility to actively take part and coordinate their own economic activities. The central government undertakes and manages only national industrial projects while the local authorities develop their own local economies, infrastructures, and public utilities.

It must be realized that in the past 18 years of reform, advances have been made where power has been decentralized and local authorities have been granted the authority to develop their local economies. This has spurred the growth of the market economy and the flourishing of the national economy as well. But it is based on local development. Some powers are still in the hands of the central government, of committees, etc. It is still a harsh fact of life that local authorities often have to run from ministry to ministry to get anything done in their own locality. This is more true with some situations than with others. In the interests of prosperity and further development it's time we resolve such contradictions.

Under a market economy the government does not directly interfere with the business of enterprise. Industries of a market competitive nature operate themselves—they are no longer an appendage of the government. The economic functions of the government break down into four activities: public service and infrastructure construction, redistribution of income, such as social security, training and education, balancing different income levels in different regions, adjusting and stabilizing the economy through macrocontrols, and finally indirect management of state assets. With those functions now clearly defined, it is easy to work out the functions of local government.

Under a market economy the government must grant a certain degree of autonomy to local governments in the area of economic management. Such autonomy is of course exercised under the leadership of the central government according to the economic guidelines it has set. Such autonomy falls under several categories.

a) Autonomy of economic adjustment.

i) Local authorities must have the right to draw up economic development plans. Such plans must dovetail with national economic development planning and reflect the actual conditions and needs of the local environment.

ii) Local authorities must also have the right of financial planning with respect to the local economy. Under the system of shared tax revenues local government should be allowed to increase or reduce minor tax schedules as they see fit. They should be allowed to mandate suitable reductions in tax rates and exemptions from local tax. They should be permitted to adjust economic supply and demand in their local areas by an increase or decrease of financial expenditures and to promote the development of local enterprises with financial subsidies and other means.

iii) Autonomy in making financial adjustments. Any locality should be permitted to set up local development banks, establish local insurance and trust companies, issue bonds or debentures, and adjust the interest rates on deposits in their banks.

iv) The locality should also have the right to adjust wages and salaries. If necessary a locality could adjust the total level of local wages and salaries by introducing a tax to guarantee a minimum wage.

v) Local government should also, in cases of urgent need,

have the right to adjust and control price levels of selected commodities by placing a price ceiling on them or adjusting supply and demand.

b) Autonomy in undertaking investment. Initiating basic construction of a region's infrastructure or public utilities requires funds. A local government must have the autonomy to raise such funds and otherwise attract capital. Stocks and bonds can be issued. Business can be invited to open subsidiaries in the region, and foreign investments and loans can be sought.

c) Autonomy in administrative management of state assets. Under ordinary circumstances local government does not directly manage state assets, and allows such enterprises to operate independently. However, local government can help push forward the reform of the state asset management system by setting up independent investment companies, holding companies, promoting the separation of administration from business management, setting up markets, reorganizing local state owned enterprises into corporations, and following the laws and guidelines to ensure that state assets are not lost or depreciate in value.

Competition should be encouraged. But the government can ensure it is fair competition. The old traditional ways of increasing and decreasing economic power at whim and improving local conditions arbitrarily should cease. Under that system there is an extreme imbalance between monies retained by enterprises, money turned over to the government, and subsidy monies. This creates controversy between central and local governments and results in unfair competition among regions.

A better method is a standardized system, using scientific principles. For example fiscal balance was maintained in the former Federal Republic of Germany. The finances of each state were computerized by means of a scientific accounting formula set by law. Financial transfers were made only according to that formula. This guaranteed justice and fairness and ensured that the rich states who showed initiative in increasing production would not be penalized. Only under such a system can regions and localities engage in fair competition amongst themselves.

A national condition of fair competition in regions and

localities should be actively promoted.

a) Local governments must not take arbitrary measures which widen the gap in the development of different regions. This will just lead to blocks in launching fair competition.

b) More help should be given to backward regions to enhance their competitive power. At the same time encouragement should be given to the more developed coastal regions to develop resources in the central and western regions and strengthen cooperation between east and west, north and south.

c) Any blockade or regional protectionism should be lifted or removed. A unified market should be set up to promote fair competition among regions.

d) Localities should be encouraged to improve investment conditions and strengthen their infrastructure in order to attract investment from outside the region.

e) In the rural areas individual and multiple ownership should be encouraged. The development of the non-government sector should be accelerated.

All these measures have as their goal bringing into full play the initiative of all regions and localities.

III. Inflation Must Be Effectively Curbed While Stepping Up Reform and Development

Inflation is a critical problem in socioeconomic life. Different opinions have been offered from different quarters as to the best way to approach this problem. Further analysis needs to be made. Inflation in China today can be attributed to the following factors: a weak agricultural foundation, an inadequate supply of agricultural and agricultural related products, lack of adequate price reform, lack of efficiency in state owned enterprises, lack of market orientation. But underlying all the above is the fact that the restructuring of the economy has not been thorough.

From 1981 to 1993 statistics show that 60 percent of the economic growth was directly due to increased investment. Investment caused this expansion. Further expansion of the Chinese economy both now and in times to come will thus largely depend on increased investment. But there is a problem at present: investments are bringing in low returns due to the inefficiency of state owned enterprises which have been the recipients of sizable investment. The solution to increased investment then is to increase the efficiency of enterprises.

Investment can stimulate inflation. Certain periods of inflation in China seem to bear out this fact. However, there are regions where investment has increased but inflation has not followed. So the problem may not be exclusively caused by investment. For instance, Hainan increased its fixed asset investment in 1990 by 23.4 percent than the previous year, in 1991 by 28.4 percent and in 1992 by a staggering 90.8 percent. However, in that same period the respective retail sales price indexes gained by only 0.6 percent, 3.1 percent, and 8.7 percent. This investment did not trigger hyper inflation. And looking over the start of economic growth in Japan, South Korea, Singapore, and Hong Kong, the annual investment increase was approximately 30 percent while retail sales prices increased below 5 percent on average. So it is clear that investment itself does not necessarily cause inflation. What is required, however, is that the investment system and corresponding finance and banking systems conform with the structure and demands of a market economy.

a) Direct investment by the state should be strictly controlled. At present direct investment by the state comprises the lion's share of the country's total investment—60-70 percent. But as reform of the investment structure has not really been implemented, the efficiency of this investment is very low. According to statistics an investment of 100 yuan in a state-owned enterprise will yield a profit of 2.7 yuan while the same amount put into a township enterprise will yield 7.2 yuan. In the period between January and June 1994, the total output of state industrial enterprises increased only 5.3 percent whereas that of collective industrial enterprises increased 27.8 percent. It is clear that the gains derived from state investments are falling far short of those from the non-public sector.

It is possible to solve this problem of direct state investment. First of all, state budgets must be strictly enforced. New projects should not be arbitrarily launched. No new organizations should be arbitrarily set up. And loans should not be granted which will lead to inflation. The total amount of paper money issued must be controlled. No expansionary credit is to be granted by banks. And those with the legal responsibility for making investments must be held accountable for the results of those investments.

b) Social programs can be furthered through investment channels. Housing reform is critical—houses should be sold to buyers at cost. Employees and workers should be encouraged to buy shares in the enterprises in which they work. Internal shares should be transferred to a workers' shareholding fund. But the scope of investment should be extended to all sorts of enterprises with strategic projects given priority.

c) Agricultural investment should be gradually expanded. The lack of investment in this area accounts for our weak agricultural base, inadequate supply of agricultural products, and soaring commodities prices. In recent years investment in agriculture has actually dropped despite an increase in total investment in China. In 1985 the amount of fixed asset investment is estimated to have been 6-7 percent. In 1990 it had dropped to 4.5 percent and in 1993 slipped further down to 3.5 percent. A key reason for this is that earnings from agricultural investments are rather low. A set of comprehensive adjustment measures is called for to resolve this problem in agricultural investment.

A successful formula for raising agricultural earnings has been found by integrating land, capital, and technology. Hainan adopted a method whereby farmers provided land, science departments provided the technology, and enterprise offered the capital. Agricultural corporations were thus formed with shares distributed according to the degree of contribution. Cooperatives could also have been set up in this way. But the result was increased investment in agriculture, and raised earnings from that investment.

B. Inflation Must Be Curbed While Price Reform is Being Implemented

Market orientation of prices cannot be accomplished in a day. And it is unavoidable to see a general rise in commodity prices during such a reform. But market orientation of price does not always directly spur a rise in price. Under adequate competitive conditions some price levels will even be cut back. In 1988 Hainan initiated reform to its grain prices. In May 1991 the purchase and selling price of grain was released from rigid state controls—the prices were allowed to fluctuate within a certain range. After this occurred the average grain price on the market did not rise but actually dropped nearly 21 percent. There was no shortage of food, no panic buying, no hoarding or fraudulent stockpiling. And this continued through 1993.

Macro management of commodity prices must be done on the basis of full competition and market orientation. Only in this way will price stability be guaranteed. But at present in China price reform is manifested by arbitrary adjustments of prices by the state. Such easily result in price chain reactions. Price levels rise and then the state must institute another artificial price adjustment. When the state raised the purchase price of agricultural products in 1993 by 13.4 percent this was followed by a rise in the price of industrial goods. The price of agricultural goods also rose by 14.1 percent. The state failed in its action and only prompted serious inflation. The answer is strengthening the competitive market, not imposing arbitrary measures.

The lack of development of infrastructure and basic industries has caused a bottleneck to economic development that must be blasted through. This problem closely relates to China's investment structure. State assets are concentrated in ordinary competitive industries, and it is the overheating in these areas which is responsible for any inflation we have seen. Meanwhile, investment in basic industries and public utilities lags far behind. State assets need to be withdrawn from ordinary competitive spheres and transferred to basic industries, public utilities, and the like to realize the optimum efficiency of these assets. Investment in ordinary competitive spheres should be made by the non-state sector including private and foreign business interests.

C. Formulate Individual Regional Policies to Control Inflation

Since the 1950s regional economic development has witnessed many breakthroughs both in theory and practice. And there have been many successes. But at the root of this problem is the existing situation that China is a very large country and there has been a very uneven development in different regions. And handling the conditions which have brought about inflation in these different locales requires different policies based on their differences in development. Each region should be allowed to formulate its own inflation control policy in line with its actual condition.

The opening up of China has been preceded by the opening up of individual regions. The priority development of these few regions led to an expansion of the development of the surrounding areas, which in turn stimulated the development of the entire economy.

Take Hainan as an example. It would have been very difficult for it to develop its economy by relying on its own accumulated capital. Its high growth occurred as a result of the huge investments it attracted from abroad. Once the island was established as a Special Economic Zone, its real estate became a blue chip investment industry. Real estate development prompted complementary development in commerce, service industries, the building industry, transport, and other related industries. It also prompted an upgrade in the infrastructure level of its cities, which in turn improved the investment conditions for the SEZ as a whole. Hainan did something quite unique, too, in making tourism a leading industry. This special policy was determined by unique geographical and historical conditions. Real estate and tourism, being closely related, complemented each other and provided conditions advantageous for the growth of each. Other provinces and areas should use this as an example.

IV. Correctly Handling the Relationships Between the Utilization of Foreign Investment and Control of Inflation

A. More Foreign Capital Must Be Used to Promote the Stable Development of the Chinese Economy

Foreign investment must be used in such a way as to not spark inflationary trends. China's strategy is to continue to open up new regions which will attract foreign capital. The setting up of foreign owned enterprises in China is also a priority as is the development of foreign trade. The Chinese national economy must gear itself to become a key player in international markets. This in turn will further stimulate China's economic growth.

International capital is always seeking the most optimum conditions for investment. Even developed countries try in many ways to attract foreign capital. But the sustained high growth of China's economy in contrast to the world's current economic recession makes China extremely attractive to foreign investment. But big changes occur in different regions. In 1990 only 12.6 billion U.S. dollars went into developing countries—in 1993 that figure had jumped eightfold to 104.8 billion U.S. dollars. In 1990 foreign capital investment in securities and bonds was 500 million U.S. dollars while three years later it had increased to 37.1 billion U.S. dollars. And between those same three years foreign capital investment in industrial projects in developing countries rose from 12.1 to 39.5 billion U.S. dollars.

If we take a broad view of developing countries we can see two potential scenarios: the first is that when foreign capital is attracted to areas it is accompanied by high inflation such as in Latin American countries. The second is that when large amounts of foreign aid have been attracted to other regions, such as Singapore and Hong Kong, no such runaway inflation has resulted.

The key is direct foreign investment. Direct foreign investment occupies a predominant role in Singapore's expansion. Although it is true that country has also attracted loans from the

World Bank, Asia Development Bank and Japan Overseas Cooperative Foundation, Singapore takes the view from beginning to end that any loans with conditions attached are not nearly as good as direct investment. In the years from 1975 to 1984 direct foreign investment constituted 97.7 percent of Singapore's long term capital flow. Both Hong Kong and South Korea have emulated this model with successful results.

In China "indirect" investment of foreign capital creates a problem in balance of payments. Large loans of money increase the amount of supply and demand of currency while "direct" investment decreases the pressure on the RMB. Let's take a look at Hainan again. From April 1988 to August 1994, 3.19 billion U.S. dollars of foreign capital flooded into that special economic zone. Of this only 6.3 percent were in the form of indirect investments and over 80 percent were direct investments. Between January and September of 1994, 568 million U.S. dollars were poured into Hainan. About 75 percent was direct investment in the form of materials of all sorts. Because of this only 200 million U.S. dollars (or 35 percent) had to be used as RMB allocation of foreign currency.

If foreign businessmen can be encouraged to make direct investments it bolsters the RMB by improving balance of payments. It is also a sign of the overall viability of the economy.

At the same time direct investment means that more attention will be paid to the rate of efficiency of capital. Foreign businessmen always seek to obtain the maximum amount of profit at the minimum cost. In addition, as a rule, large foreign corporations and conglomerates have tended to target large projects that promise better and more stable investment returns. Towards that end, such businessmen favor China's major infrastructure projects for their investments.

Accordingly, we should adopt a more open policy and remove artificial limitations placed on foreign investment. Unnecessary constraints in allocating stocks should also be eradicated.

In order to guide foreign capital to invest in the direction of the best interests of China's long term development, favorable treatment in terms of credits and tax breaks should be offered.

These would apply to such projects as basic industries, infrastructure and high tech, and particularly energy and transportation.

One of China's main objectives in using foreign capital is to promote the development of its foreign trade. The simple formula is that superior product and efficiency will produce superior profits, both at home and in international markets. In absorbing U.S., Japanese, and European capital, the "four small dragons" (Hong Kong, Taiwan, Singapore and South Korea) of Asia seized the opportunity to readjust the world's industrial structure by integrating international capital with their abundant material resources and cheap labor. Their recently created industries and export led economy thus have a strong competitive edge.

At this writing the import-export quota for foreign-invested enterprises is only one third of the total. If we firmly persist in the strategy of using foreign capital to develop export-led business, we can surely strengthen the competitive power of Chinese products and use this to promote the stable development of the Chinese economy.

B. We Must Carefully Monitor the Impact of the Inflow of Large Amounts of Foreign Capital and Seek Positive Ways to Control Any Tendency Towards Inflation

The amount of foreign capital coming into China in recent years has increased tremendously. In 1993, it reached 36.77 billion U.S. dollars. In the first eight months of 1994 direct investment by foreign businessmen reached 20.4 billion U.S. dollars. This caused an overheating of the economy and to a certain extent resulted in inflation.

But looking at the in-flow of capital is not enough. We must also look at its out-flow which in today's China is a serious problem. It is estimated that over 200 billion U.S. dollars have left China and gone abroad through various channels. A precise policy needs to be drawn up by the Chinese government to restrict this out-flow and standardize related procedures.

Foreign businessmen should be accorded the same treatment as Chinese citizens as regards investments. The policy of giving preferential treatment to foreign businessmen so as to attract foreign investment in China was a necessary step for a certain period of time, but as the transition to a market economy is being speeded up foreign invested and Chinese enterprises should be given equal opportunity to compete with each other, otherwise conditions will tend to tempt capital to flee from China to abroad.

But while direct investment in export-led business must be encouraged, controls should be placed on foreign capital entering into speculative business in China. Such speculation can only lead to unwanted economic fluctuations. Strategies must be worked out and policy drafted which effectively deals with this problem.

V. Suggestions on Effective Control of Inflation

In view of the fact that present rates of inflation are still within an acceptable level. The economic growth rate should be maintained at 10 percent in 1995. Last year the supply of over 90 percent of consumer goods met their demand—in other words a balance was reached in the mechanics of supply and demand for these goods. No panicky buying occurred as in 1988.

Since 1979 China's yearly economic growth has averaged 9.3 percent with an annual increase of 6.44 percent rise in retail commodity prices. The growth rate should be maintained at over 9 percent in the coming few years. If it were to drop lower than 8 percent aside from the losses that would result we would see a suspension of production, overstocking of products, and serious unemployment—it could endanger social stability. However, with the growth rate continued at 9-10 percent the excellent development trend of the national economy can be continued.

The rather high rate of inflation which did occur in 1994 was mainly due to the readjustment of commodity prices—the relaxation of controls, reform in the wages of civil servants, standardization of exchange rates, and tax reform and excessive investment in fixed assets. During this stage of readjusting the economy it is difficult to completely avoid a rise in the general level of commodity prices. These matters are not to be regarded lightly but neither need we be alarmed. This is the cost we must pay for reform. And by accelerating and perfecting reform measures we can certainly remove the structural root causes that give rise to inflation. In the meantime, while promoting a gradual market orientation we can nonetheless preserve stability and do everything possible to curb inflation.

Inflation and standard of living. A relatively high inflation rate would reduce the standard of living of a considerable number of people as wages (and particularly pensions) will have a hard time keeping up with price rises. State owned enterprises which are in financial difficulties or whose production has been poor will have difficulties in paying the wages, salaries, and pensions to their employees, workers and retirees. The social hardships this would cause could provoke strong reactions from the people. In our work then we must make the curbing of inflation an important aim of macro control to prevent inflation from playing havoc with the social and economic relations of the country.

It is necessary and feasible to bring inflation down to 15 percent in 1995 while at the same time accelerating reform. This year we have removed many of the key factors which gave rise to this inflation, so the inflationary pressures next year will be relaxed. With the correct measures taken, this 15 percent target can be met.

The first measure that must be undertaken to curb inflation is the control of the prices of agricultural and related products. This can be best done through efforts to increase agricultural production and ensure that an abundant supply of such produce reaches the market. The most outstanding feature of the 1994 inflation was the high rise in the prices of farm produce. Between January and August of that year retail food prices rose 60 percent. The three main food staples—rice, wheat and corn—rose 84.7 percent, 48.8 percent and 40.1 percent respectively compared to the same period in the previous year. These rises prompted further rises in fodder, meat, fowl and eggs. In present day China workers and employees spend over half their wages and salaries on basic living expenses. Excessively high price rises in farm products, then, impact greatly on the daily life of the people. Once the government ceases its various price support and subsidy programs which have been artificially keeping down the retail cost of these goods, any shortages will inevitably cause prices to rise. Thus an abundance of these agricultural goods is the best guarantee of keeping their prices at a reasonable and acceptable level.

The reduction or loss of cultivated land should be strictly controlled to prevent any drop in rice production from the southeastern coastal provinces. Conflicts and differences in strains and quality of foodstuffs will be solved in the marketplace.

Adjustment must be made to raise the price of rice above that of flour. In China's cities and towns much more rice is consumed than any other grain (60-65 percent of total grain consumption). This percentage continues to increase. At the same time, the main rice producing areas in South China demonstrate a distinct lack of enthusiasm at growing food at low profits. But when rice is in short supply, the entire market contracts. To ensure increased rice output we must take effective measures to control the reduction of cultivated land and at the same time made suitable adjustments between rice and other foodstuffs. The system of compensating farmers who plant rice should be strengthened.

But farmers in North China should also be encouraged to grow rice. The quality of rice grown in the north is excellent and can meet the demands of both the North and East China as well. An increase in the output of rice production in North China will play an important role in remedying any shortage of supply of good quality rice in North and East China.

International markets should be used to further adjust the supply and demand of rice in China. The developed southeast coastal provinces which have the ability to pay foreign exchange should be encouraged to increase their rice imports from abroad for their own consumption. Current market price for the early season paddy is 1400-1600 RMB per ton in Zhujiang Delta in Guangdong. The middle and late season paddy of good quality is 1700-2400 RMB per ton. In terms of husked rice the difference in price is 2000-2300 as compared to 2350-3300 RMB per ton. If these southern provinces have the ability to pay foreign exchange, it pays them to increase rice imports from abroad.

The state should contract the purchase of 50 million tons of grain from farmers in such a way as to guarantee the quality of the rice. The previous low price fixed by government in the purchase of grain from farmers led to many contradictions. Farmers were unwilling to sell grain to the government. Government was only willing to buy low quality grain from farmers. High commissions going to "middlemen" were taking money away from food producers and resulting in unreasonable differences between the government's purchase and sale prices. The discrepancy between China's domestic grain prices and those on the international market was being kept artificially exaggerated. For these reasons the present system governing the purchase and sale of grain by the state should be totally dismantled.

The above principles also apply to government price controls on cotton which should be similarly lifted.

But investment in agriculture is the key to remedying these situations. Inadequate attention to this sector has seriously hampered the development of agriculture in China. In relation to the total investment in capital construction, agricultural investment has been dropping. The price parity between industrial goods and agricultural goods has continued to widen in recent years. Government bodies at all echelons have been giving attention and investment to industry at the expense of agriculture, particularly in the economically better developed regions.

This frame of mind is an objective reality but one that must change. Understanding must be reached on the need to make increased agricultural investments, particularly in the areas of science and technology as applied to agronomy.

Fluctuations in foreign exchange and foreign exchange reserves has had direct impact on inflation. Measures must be taken to reduce such pressures. In 1993 an uncontrolled foreign exchange rate prompted a general rise in prices. Early in that year the Yuan was 6.8 against the U.S. Dollar. By mid '93 this had gone up to 10. The government took measures and this rate quickly dropped back to the earlier level. But the violent fluctuation adversely affected the people's confidence in the RMB which resulted in still further increases in the price of commodities.

Those fluctuations also caused the prices of imported goods to rise. But even after the exchange rate had been stably returned to its former level, it was not possible to fully revert the prices of those foreign goods. The resultant increase in the cost of important capital goods and machinery equipment ensured further increases in commodity prices.

Lastly, China now has by far too much foreign reserves. This gives rise to an increased supply of paper currency because RMB must meet the demands of these foreign reserves. As much as 67 percent of newly issued paper money in China is printed for this purpose. Thus the excess of foreign reserves accelerates the pressure towards domestic inflation.

The government must adopt a policy to stabilize the foreign exchange rate and strengthen the RMB. The exchange rate must be maintained at a reasonable level so that the RMB can ultimately become a fully convertible currency.

Under ordinary circumstances an inflation rate at home which is higher than abroad can be expected to worsen exchange rates. Recently in China, however, the reverse has been the case. In the short term, the appreciation of the RMB will act to curb inflation. In the long term, however, in the presence of continued inflation it is bound to have a reverse effect. A strong RMB increases the cost of the production of export goods which will tend to lower the exchange rate and cause the flight of capital out of the country. In the end it will result in the reduction of foreign reserves and perhaps in the depreciation of the RMB as well.

Foreign exchange controls must be reinforced and loopholes in the foreign exchange market closed. To reduce foreign currency reserves and make sure that RMB is the only acceptable means of payment, Hong Kong and U.S. dollars should be forbidden use in such transactions. Control should be exercised on the buying and selling of foreign exchange by domestic enterprises. Settlement of foreign exchange should not be allowed to increase and should be controlled as foreign exchange reserves are made to decrease. Existing capital in foreign exchange should not be permitted to be left there idle in a wasteful condition. Nor should it be allowed, unsupervised, to leave the country in bulk.

A standard foreign exchange market should be promptly established. The "foreign exchange adjustment market" and the "interbank foreign exchange market" should be unified into a single system. If not unified, then the "foreign exchange adjustment market" should be gradually abolished while the interbank market is developed.

Conditions must be created to make the RMB fully convertible to foreign exchange. For this to occur we must lift the restriction on the supply of foreign exchange to non-trade items. RMB accounts can then be allowed to fully convert to foreign exchange. To accomplish this the reform of the banking system and the strengthening of the central bank must be stepped up. This includes the further development of the capital and foreign exchange markets plus the establishment of an international banking center that will attract the deposit of foreign capital into Chinese banks.

International exchange can and should be utilized to adjust domestic markets. With the present international balance of payments and China's strong foreign exchange reserves, we should consider relaxing restrictions on imports as a means of adjusting domestic supply and demand. Fundamentally, inflation is caused by discrepancies between supply and demand. If by means of international exchange we can make up for any short-falls on the domestic market, we can effectively curb inflation. Careful strategic planning can be used to guide the importation of raw materials, semi-processed goods, and parts of finished products which are in short supply. Such planning must be forward looking and flexible. Under conditions of strong foreign exchange reserves there is no danger in lifting restrictions on certain imports.

The reform of the foreign trade system should be accelerated. To further its development, the scope of foreign trade should be enlarged and the right to engage in foreign trade should be vested in enterprises. Ordinary import-export restrictions should be abolished and bids on import and export quotas should be tendered in public or at auction.

However, our export policy must also include the prevention

of the outflow of vital resources. The export of raw materials and primary goods (particularly those in short supply) should be strictly controlled. The export of high value-added processed goods, however, should be encouraged.

A stable monetary policy must be maintained. The money supply must be controlled. In essence, inflation is a currency problem. The current inflation is the result of the excessive currency issued between 1990 and 1992. In these years the GNP increased 50 percent nominally while the yearly balance of M2 increased 108 percent (more than double). The central bank must be guaranteed relative independence to deal with this problem. As the monetary control department it must have supreme authority to counter any pressure from government or enterprises over the implementation of monetary policy. In view of the fact that the growth in the money supply has been well in excess of that of the GNP, the adjustment target for M1 and M2 should be fixed between 20-25 percent.

Bank interest rates should be market oriented. The leverage of interest rates is capable of adjusting the macro economy, stabilizing currency, limiting investment, and curbing inflation. Interest rates should therefore be freed up to float, within the guidelines of government policy, according to market supply and demand. Current interest rates on state loans is less than the rate of inflation. This has led to corruption and other financial irregularities. For this reason the interest rates on loans should be raised appropriately.

The proportion of state loans to the non-government sector should be increased in the interests of optimizing the use of bank capital. The high growth of the Chinese economy is largely the result of growth in the private sector. Yet 80 percent of bank loans are granted to state-owned enterprises which bring in low investment returns. A change in policy is therefore called for. Loans should be refused to state-owned enterprises which have continued low economic performance, whose assets are incapable of meeting liabilities, and who's future business prospects are poor. Cutting off such loans will tend to make these failing businesses either reform or reorganize themselves. Loans to non-government businesses can be extended at the same time to help them develop more quickly which will positively impact on and stimulate the growth of the entire Chinese economy.

If China's financial deficit grows too large it will directly influence inflation. Deficit financing must therefore be brought under control. The present inflation is largely related to financial deficit. In 1984-1993 accumulated deficit reached 112.826 billion RMB. This deficit, being compensated by bank overdrafts, force the central bank into monetary expansion. The scale of such overdrafts should be strictly controlled. The budget deficit should be cut down to under 3 percent of the GDP. Efforts must be made to increase financial income while limiting expenditures.

Tax agencies at both national and local levels must be streamlined. Reform must be carried out in collection and management of taxes. A system should be initiated where individuals and enterprises are responsible for personally filing and paying their taxes. Heavy penalties should be meted out to "tax dodgers." (And tax "exemptions" and "reductions" should be strictly monitored.)

Wage increases must be linked to commensurate increases in productivity. Large arbitrary wage hikes must be controlled. Although China's total wages in 1994 were scheduled to rise 18.4 percent, the actual wage increase turned out to be 30 percent, largest increase in many years. Extra pay in state owned departments (in addition to wages) registered an even faster growth —the equivalent of 1/3 of wages. In some cases it exceeded the amount of wages. Yet labor productivity in state-owned enterprise registered only an 8 percent improvement. The rise in wages brought with it higher consumer costs and an increase in the overall cost of living index.

Short term consumer spending should be channelled into longer term investment. For example, if housing reform were stepped up and the houses sold to buyers at cost, this would reduce short term consumption. It would also reduce bank credits on housing construction and tend to make housing funds self perpetuating. Employees of enterprises should be encouraged to buy enterprise stocks. Employee stock-holding programmes can be instituted on a voluntary basis.

The bottom line in controlling inflation, however, is the continued reform of state owned enterprises. The biggest contradiction in our economy is the disparity between the high degree of investment in state-owned enterprises (over 80 percent) and the low returns from such investments. With such low efficiency these state-owned enterprises are unable to cope with structural price rises such as price rises in agricultural products. They ride on the bandwagon of price rises, but due to their serious losses and shortages of capital they actually prevent bank interest rates from being adjusted upwards. Since this makes it impossible to bring investment under control of market guidelines, the total volume of money cannot be controlled either. Therefore we can see that state-owned enterprises constitute the biggest reasons for inflation. By reforming state-owned enterprises we can reverse the situation of high investments—low yields. If this is not remedied the economy can do nothing but stagnate.

Some immediate steps that should be taken include gradually allowing bankrupt state operated enterprises to actually declare bankruptcy. This would only include those who have been making losses over a long period of time, with assets below debts and with poor or no production. Such must not be done to affect social stability, however. Smaller state operated enterprises can be turned into non-government enterprises to be operated by private individuals or can maintain state owned status, but can become productive through such means as stock selling, leasing, selling, etc. Ordinary medium-sized operations should be granted autonomy of operation and become responsible for their own profit and loss. Such will either survive or go bankrupt. The few big state operated enterprises should be changed over to corporate status and structure to prevent any further waste of society's resources. The aim here is to rapidly restructure state owned enterprises to an optimum pattern and efficiency clearly raised. In this way the difficulties they face can be solved and instead of causing inflationary pressure they can be the main force in eradicating it.

Keeping the public informed is important in preventing

inflation. The People's Bank of China should regularly make public its money supply as well as its target price and current programs being implemented to curb inflation. The results of broad economic and social surveys should also be revealed to the public from time to time to keep them briefed. The government, in doing so, will prompt greater coordination with various publics on inflation issues and remove misunderstandings and eradicate the effects of false rumours.

The reform of the statistical system should also be carried out. Statistical laws should be strictly adhered to. Statistical agencies should be kept independent and scientific in their analyses, procedures and reports.

Chapter III
Rural Economic Reform
in China's Economic Transition

China's transition from a planned economy to a market economy is, in a sense, a transition from the traditional agricultural economy to a modern industrialized economy. Therefore, the transformation which bears the most fundamental and long-term significance is the reform of the rural economy in establishing markets. This may be the singular most important part of China's overall economic reform.

This is a practical as well as a pressing issue. In the special transitional period, it is imperative to be soberly aware that rural reform should not be neglected and the deepening of that reform should take precedence above all other measures. At present, the major theoretical and practical questions that need immediate resolution are: how to turn the development of the rural land use system firmly in the direction of the shareholding system while guaranteeing long term stability and prosperity; how to accelerate the process of putting agricultural produce under market economy; how to maintain a coordinated development between the rural and urban market economies so as to ensure a proper rural-urban relationship.

I. The Pressing Tasks That the
Rural Reform Faces in the
Transitional Period

After the Third Plenum of the Central Committee of the Eleventh National Congress of the Chinese Communist Party, the countryside took the lead in the reform and made notable advances. More than a decade of reform has vigorously promoted the development of agriculture and the rural economy, brought about historical changes to the countryside and laid down an important foundation for the reform and development of the national economy as a whole. Generally speaking, rural areas in China are still in the transitional process from a planned economic system to socialist market economy, so the tasks of reform are far from being completed. The contradictions and problems in the economic operations of rural areas that have emerged in the recent transitional period have been complicated ones and of a unique nature.

A. The Actual Position of the Rural Reform and Development in the Macro Stability

The establishment of a socialist market economy system depends upon a stable social environment. About 80 percent of China's population resides in the countryside. Hence, the stability of this social environment relies on the stability of agriculture and the countryside. Practice in past years has proven that once agriculture consolidated and the countryside stabilized, China saw increased stability, the economic transition became more smoothly implemented, and the national economy became better sustained with a more rapid and healthy development.

Fundamentally speaking, the lack of alignment of the rural economy with a balanced national economy stemmed from the traditional planned economic system. In the past, China's socialist economic construction placed stress and priority on heavy industry.

Therefore, it was necessary to maintain a high production of agricultural products while keeping these products in an artificially low price. This depressed the income level of agricultural workers while also lowering wages and costs in other industries as well. All for the sake of increased industrial output. Agricultural produce being the raw material not only for the food industry but also for most light industry as well, you could say it was the cornerstone of the whole planned economy. And the state,

95

with its monopoly over the purchase and marketing of all this produce could and did easily keep the prices very low. However, when, through reform, the rural economy outgrew its earlier role of merely providing food and clothing, and began to also assist the industrial sector and advance into the arena of the market economy, the earlier macroeconomic controls were shaken from their roots. At that time we saw cities which were primed with state-owned enterprises lagging behind the rural areas where non-state-owned economy became the mainstay.

The problem was that it was impossible for industry and commerce in low level markets to smoothly digest agricultural produce whose prices were being adjusted upwards through the mechanisms of the market. China has been going back and forth in the imbalance between urban and rural reform since the mid-80s. The dilemma lingers on. The urban system finds it hard to accept the acceleration of rural market upgrades while the farmers' enthusiasm to produce is dampened if their income is reduced and their difficulties go unsolved due to a slowdown of that same reform.

Earlier policy in this area has become outmoded and ineffective.

B. How to Push Forward the Reform of Purchase and Marketing of Products Under the Pressure of Inflation

China has now carried out reform in the purchase and marketing of products several times. The most recent one started in early 1993. One place after another announced the abolition of contracted purchase of grain and most cities and towns abandoned supplying grain at parity price. Instead the purchase and marketing of grain was opened up to the market. The central government work conference held in the same year put forward the measure of "guarantee the quantity and open the price control," that is, the original purchase quotas do not change while the price floats according to market need. By the year's end, grain prices rose sharply, so the government continued to practice contracted purchase at the price fixed by the central government and explicitly requested the grain department to purchase 80 billion *jin* of grain at negotiated prices in addition to the contracted purchase of 100 billion *jin*, so as to control the source of grain. After the autumn harvest of 1994, the prices for grain and cotton again climbed up, a most striking phenomenon in the nationwide inflation. Under this situation, the central government had to demand that state-owned grain departments place a price ceiling on the sales of basic grain ration and emphasized that grain-buyers should not purchase grain directly from the countryside, but at the whole sale grain markets above county level. In view of this, cities and towns in some places resumed the practice of using ration coupons for basic daily consumption of grain. Some of them even closed grain markets and restricted sales within certain regions or areas, thus causing reversals in market reform.

Any attempt to reform the traditional system of purchase and marketing of agricultural products poses a number of questions which are worth discussing.

First, how do you correctly estimate the balance supply and demand of basic agricultural produce like cotton and grain. Different estimates will lead to different production quotas. According to the experience of the last few years, a shortage in the supply of products caused pessimistic estimates to prevail as public opinion sought to change policy decision making. The other side of the coin occurred whenever there was an abundant supply of grain within a stable price range—at those times optimistic estimates would be broadly accepted. Since an accurate estimation of potential supply and demand was linked with the orientation of the reform, any discussion of the reform had to deal with scientific estimation of the prospect of a medium and long-term balanced produce supply. Particularly questions like how to assess the relationship between rapid industrialization, modernization and family-run farming, and how to assess the possibility of China's utilization of international produce markets and the protection of its borders were extremely difficult academic issues. Hundreds of schools of thought need to be pulled together to make a reliable judgement.

Secondly, how do you analyze the relation between inflation in the transitional period and the reform of produce supply and marketing. Apparently, the current rise of food prices in big and medium-sized cities played an important role in the rise of the consumer price index, about 60 percent of the contributing factor. But there are two distinct schools of thought here. One believes that the current inflation was triggered by the rise of produce prices. In order to avoid all-round galloping inflation and obtain stability, so this school argues, it is necessary to control products prices and at certain points increase supply by beefing up production. Reform of family-sized farming is seen as the tool with which to accomplish this. The other school, however, puts forward the belief that the current inflation is mainly a systematic one, that is, one caused by increasing money supply in circulation. This fact was stated to loom over every other economic aspect.

It is only because the supply and marketing of agricultural products has been relatively unresponsive to market forces that prices shot up so fast. This is a carry over from the old planned economy days. This kind of inflation can only be controlled by speeding up the reform of governmental departments. Purely administrative measures to control products prices will not remedy an imbalance of supply and demand, but rather will have a detrimental influence on attempts to balance the macro-economy.

Thirdly, is the question of whether it is possible to continue to push the reform during periods of inflation. According to a recent decision by the State Council, the responsibility for the purchase and sale of grain, cotton and fertilizer for the year of 1994 was placed in the laps of the governors and mayors. Provinces and cities were given the freedom to try and balance their supply and marketing of food products and other raw materials through inter-provincial, inter-city and even international markets. This was a big step forward over the previous year, 1993, when the central government controlled the source of grain through a centralized grain department. Here the central government was requesting provinces and cities to keep a balanced supply and marketing of products transactions for 1994, no matter what approach they might choose to adopt. Of course, there was always possibility that the governors or mayors might simply rely on old administrative procedures such as enforcing purchasing quotas, to disrupt price mechanisms and even block the regional trade. Therefore, how to strive for the former opportunity and avoid the latter possibility became a focus in practical policy research.

C. How to Face the Shift of Rural Manpower to Non-Agricultural Industries and into Cities and Towns

The transfer of surplus rural manpower poses another striking problem in China's economic transitional period. China has a large population with less land and fewer employment opportunities. It is estimated that China's surplus rural manpower now numbers between 100 and 120 million with an annual increase projected of 6 to 7 million. Along with the adjustment of agricultural structure and the development of agricultural modernization, the shift of surplus manpower to non-agricultural industries and into urban areas has become a common phenomenon in the process of industrialization in many other countries of the world as well.

The improvement of farmers' income directly influences the effective purchasing power at domestic markets. At present, it is an imperative task for the national economy to control inflation. But we should not forget the quite serious situation that many industries are operating under capacity. The fact is that the national economy has been in a slump in the past few years. Low efficiency in the state-owned enterprises is one cause while the slow increase of farmers' income denying them the incentive to produce more is another cause.

The shift of the abundant surplus rural manpower has indeed brought about many challenges to the society. There are two key economic questions we must raise here. One is whether the sharp increase of non-agricultural employment will lead to a general rise in commodity prices as a result of a rapid increase in the cost of agricultural production. The other is whether the national economic structure, in particular the industrial and urban sectors, is capable of utilizing such a huge volume of redundant rural manpower for re-employment. We should also see that the shift of farmers' employment is interwoven with the unbalanced development between different regions. China's rural manpower is mainly flowing not only from agriculture to non-agriculture, from the rural to the urban but also from less developed areas to developed areas. It is still unclear how it would influence the income balance in different regions.

D. How to Establish Grass-Roots Social Organizations That Are Amenable to Smooth Transition

Village organization has been the weakest link in the transition of China's economic system. In the years of the people's communes, the mechanism of administrative mobilization of rural resources went deep into villages. After the reform, the Constitution stipulated that villages should be self-governing. But as to how far that self government should extend there has been no set standard or guide. In recent years, there were many outstanding problems related to the very weak structure of village organization, such as the heavy burden on farmers, tense relationship between cadres and the masses and the decaying management of public affairs in some village areas.

The structure of village organization is an important element of the rural market economy. In the first place, the village as the most fundamental rural organization, serve as the link and bridge that translate central government policy and guidelines into actual action. We are here talking about the production of farmers who number in the hundreds of millions. Secondly, village organizations as farmers' self-governing organization, should uphold the state and collective interests as well as speak for farmers and serve their interests. Thirdly, in market economy, village organizations serve as representative of the collective owners of farmland and function to stabilize and adjust the right to contract land. Thus, how to strengthen village organization construction is an important and urgent subject in deepening of rural economic reform. It is one which needs deeper study by the academic and theoretical sectors.

At present village organizations are in the midst of a transformation between an old system and a new. They are on a sharp edge of contradictory points of reform, sandwiched in between the government and the farmers. There are lots of difficulties. That there is no systematic financial foundation at village level has been a hidden block to long-term stability in the rural society. How to establish a stable financial foundation of a self-governing village amidst currrent financial and tax reform is a major problem that must be solved to achieve overall political and economic stability.

II. The Key to Deepening the Reform of the Property Right System in the Countryside Is the Promotion of the Systematized Long-Term Utilization of Farmland

A. Farmland Utilization Is the Major Problem in the General Development of Rural Areas

In the 80s, the most far-reaching and progressive factor in China's reform of the countryside was the institution of the family responsibility system. Through legal contracts families were made responsible for the land they operated and for the first time remuneration became linked to production. Granting this right engendered the enthusiasm of a vast number of farmers—it suddenly paid to produce more—and as a result overall production tremendously increased.

In the past few years the contracting period was extended and property rights reform for the first time permitted the transference of land use rights. These measures played a very positive role but they failed to fully sort out all the contradictions inherent in this property rights issue. Some of the main ones which stood out in the last few years are as follows:

1) The increase of non-agricultural uses of farmland became a major problem. While arable land for grain-growing was decreasing grain itself was in increasingly short supply. "Development Zone" fever and "real estate" fever started a large-scale "enclosure movement," which drastically reduced cultivated land. In each of the past two years China lost over 800,000 acres of cultivated land. In one third of all provinces and autonomous

regions the per capita average of arable land dropped to less than 0.15 of an acre.

In today's China 275 million acres is the irreducible minimum area of cultivated land required to guarantee basic grain production quotas. Anything less portends danger. By 1992 cultivated farmland had already fallen to less than 285 million and the following year it diminished by a further 2 million acres. In 1994 it fell below the danger level—down to 270 million acres. In nineteen provinces cultivated land for grain production has decreased. Presently China's per capita cultivated land is less than 1/5 of an acre—about one quarter of the world's average. This situation gets more and more serious with the continued sharp reduction of arable land.

2) Arbitrary adjustment of farmland have become more and more frequent. Per current policy the collective owns the land, the family contracted responsibility system was to be stabilized and perfected, the initial 15-years of contractual period was extended for another 30 years. Per this same policy contractual relations would not be adjusted due to changes in household members during the contractual period and priced subcontracting was even allowed.

Because farmland under the responsibility system had originally been distributed according to the number in each household, it was requested that such land be redistributed to reflect the increase or decrease of households members. In the past two years, many places used this as an excuse to frequently adjust farmland allocations for shorter time spans on the account of the changes in households' members. This resulted in a general increase in the non-agricultural use of farmland. The central government's principle of "general stability and minor adjustment" was used as a justification for frequent adjustment of farmland though this was not the intent of this policy. From one viewpoint it might only seem to be a "minor adjustment" but overall these frequent "minor tremors" have served to unstabilize the family responsibility system and the investment expectation of farmers.

3) Agricultural investment in terms of manpower, funding and technology has decreased. Farmers' investment in farmland

has been on a striking decline. In 1994, overall agricultural investment went from the previous year's 2.8 percent down to 2.2 percent. In the past two years, uncertainty concerning a farmer's exact property rights over the land he tilled generated insecurity and other negative backlash including a drop in efficiency in grain production. The economic climate had sharply dampened the enthusiasm for farmers to invest in agriculture. Instead they diversified and channeled the bulk of their formerly agricultural funds into urban or non-agricultural industries. At the same time large numbers of trained agricultural technical personnel were leaving their jobs for more lucrative positions in other fields.

The foundation of agricultural development and rural stability is farmland. In deepening rural reform and accelerating the process of establishing rural markets, it is imperative to be bolder in advancing the reform so as to better utilize this farmland. This includes laying down a solid foundation for rural property right relationship.

B. The Reform of the Property Right System with Respect to Farmland Must Move Forward, and the Enthusiasm of Farmers Must Be Revitalized

1) A codified farmland property rights system must exist to provide rules and regulations which clearly outline rights and restrictions concerning farmland. Since collective ownership will continue, stipulating various property rights and limits and clarifying the relationship between the right to own and the right of use will go a long way toward making farmland utilization more efficient. Standardizing regulatory procedures is also a part of this.

2) Bit obstacles to farmers who might increase investment in agriculture are the ambiguous nature of rural real estate rights and the frequent changes in operating rights. The family responsibility system adjusted, to a certain extent, the relations between farmers and the farmland and initiated farmers' enthusiasm but it did not clarify the legal property relations between the farmer and his land. Ownership is still unclear, the right to use unstable —and these, added to the frequent "readjustment" of farmland

allocation have made farmers reluctant to increase investment, particularly in medium and long term investments.

3) As the fundamental goal in reforming the farmland system is the revitalization of the rural economy, any innovation that could improve rural productivity might be given a try.

C. The Establishment of a Shareholding System Should Be Undertaken as the Main Action in Advancing Farmland System Reform

To legalize farmers' extended right to use farmland. Though the central government clearly stipulates that another 30 years will be added to any extant farmland contracts, farmers may still lack security concerning their long term prospects. Therefore, it would be preferable confirm farmers' long-term right to use the farmland by legislation than to simply announce the policy will remain unchanged for 30 more years. New legislation would reassure the farmers by clearly defining and protecting their rights and interests. A farmer must be confident that as the possessor of his farmland he has the full right to use, transfer and rent farmland plus pass it on to his successor. Guaranteeing these privileges by law will go far to preventing farmland acreage from being further divided. It will also make farmers much more responsible for the land and its yield. All this is conducive to guiding agricultural producers' long-term actions in a very positive direction.

The realization of farmers' long-term right to use farmland will encourage them to make medium and long term investments in that farmland.

At present, 60 percent of total agricultural investment comes from farmers, 20 percent from local and communal economy and only 20 percent from the government, which is supposed to increase agricultural investment every year. But the major investors are farmers themselves. A farmer's desire to invest comes from the expected gains to be made from his farming. These expectations need encouragement from the system. The most decisive statement would be an explicit definition of the farmer's long-term rights in respect to his farmland. This would encourage him to put more work, funds and technology into his farming to ensure increased future yields from his labors.

Instituting the shareholding system for farmland is the best choice for accelerating and deepening rural reform. It also solves a number of related problems.

First, such a system would encourage farmers to turn their long-term utilization rights into shares. As shareholders they would join or form various kinds of co-operative organizations, agricultural development projects and larger scale economic ventures and, of course, receive regular dividends according to how many shares they hold.

Secondly, it would facilitate the transfer and consolidation of farmland and the use of rural surplus manpower.

At present, rural surplus manpower fall roughly into two categories. The first is comprised of those laborers who have branched off from agriculture but remained in the countryside, often working in township-run enterprises and on contracted farmland.

The second consists of those who migrate to cities. These would not wish to lose their rural benefits (namely the right to contract farmland) particularly when their status makes them ineligible for the exclusive urban benefits. So deriving an income by living and working in cities, while at the same time contracting farm land in the country is a common substitute for social security benefits in the current economic system. What do they do with their farm land? Often giving it to others to grow grain on their behalf. That farmers do not want to lose their farmland essentially means that they do not want to lose the security such can afford them. This poses an obstacle to the transfer of farmland.

The goal of agricultural modernization is to transform the current small-scale, individual and dispersed agricultural management into large-scale, modern, labor intensive and efficient management and socialized services, to strive for upgrading labor productivity and farmland output, to increase farmers' income and to inject new vigor into agriculture.

The main approach to farmland shareholding is the establishment of shareholding agricultural cooperative enterprises to improve overall management of the farmland. This works as follows. Individual plots of farmland that have been contracted to households merge into a cooperative venture. The enterprise's rationed grain as well as its net profits will be distributed on the basis of proportionate ownership of the total stock of the company. The shareholders of these agricultural enterprises may themselves work in the company or employ non-shareholders to work in their stead.

The share is a certificate which a farmer holds in exchange for transferring his contract (the right to use the farmland) to the shareholding cooperative. With this certificate he obtains rationed grain (according to basic standard) and dividends from the cooperative enterprises. In this way, the right to use farmland can be circulated entirely according to market principles. Large-scale management, high yield and economic efficiency on the farm can be achieved in this wise.

Farmland shareholding cooperative enterprises will enable farmers to benefit from any shift of farmland from agricultural to non-agricultural use and increase their income to some extent.

It is unavoidable that some farmland be used for non-agricultural purpose in the process of industrialization. Industrial enterprises, development zones and public transportation facilities will at times require such land.

Presently at the time of the requisition of such land, the farmer holding the right to use it will get a lump sum compensation, which is often not enough to cover the long-term losses he will suffer from the lost of farmland. This often acts as an infringement or deprivation of farmers rights.

But if dealing with an agricultural cooperative, in the changing of farmland to non-agriculatural use, it is only necessary to negotiate the initial price plus future dividends. The shareholding farmers, in return for surrendering their rights to personally use that land, will receive not only immediate benefits but future income as well. So, while advancing the process of industrialization farmers will also secure a stable and increasing income to assist in bridging the gap between the urban and rural economies.

D. Actively Nurturing the Land Market in the Countryside

Land allocations cannot be continually altered every time the number of family members changes. It is imperative to contain further division and redistribution of farmland in China's countryside. According to the current system, so long as one resides in the community, no matter whether a new-born or a newly-arrive member through marriage, he or she enjoys the legal right to use or contract a piece of farmland. This creates continuous redivision and redistribution of the land. The practice of "neither more land for more family members nor less land for fewer family members" should be encouraged and regulated by policy, so as to keep the land reform developing in a more standard direction.

The experiment of "two categories of farmland" may be expanded. Whereas cultivated land was distributed strictly on a per capita basis in most places, Pingdu City in Shandong experimented with an alternative method which should be considered for export to other places.

In Pingdu each farmer was given the same basic share from a small part of the collective land. This equally distributed share (farmland for rationed grain) met the farmers' basic need. No collective fund or tax was levied from it.

The larger portion of land, however, was distributed through competitive bidding. All taxes and involuntary contributions to the village came from the production of this section of land, called the responsibility farmland.

E. Stabilizing and Using the Family Responsibility System as the Basis to Develop Large-Scale Agricultural Production

The most important and fundamental rural reform to date is the universal establishment of a household contract responsibility system linking remuneration to production. This has opened up new areas for the revival and development of the family economy in both rural and urban China. Where this system is strongly supported that area's productivity is strong and vigorous. It is the basis for future expansion in the direction of large-scale production.

The attainment of large-scale agricultural production will be the result of a long historical process that will reflect the existing situation of China's economy and its productive resources. It will roughly go through the following stages:

First is the conventional agricultural period. The investment of production factors consists mainly of farmland and manpower, with a very large proportion of self-sufficient production. Farmland is not only something the farmer relies on for making a living but also something to provide social security and welfare. The whole society is right now in the initial stage of developing into an industrialized country from an agricultural one. Employment opportunities are narrow. The cost of modernization is high while current labor efficiency is very low. In this stage, the most usual farming organizational forms are small farm enterprises with family farming as the basis. In these circumstances it is difficult and uneconomical to force the merger of semi-self-sufficient small farmers in order to establish collective ventures.

The second stage sees the merger of these semi-self-sufficient agricultural units into larger structures. At this stage family farming is still the main productive force but socialized services for production have been separated out to reduce expenses on trading deals and to improve service quality. At this time, agricultural cooperative organizations and other commercial organizations are developing and thriving in response to the emerging needs to provide pre-production and post-production services.

The third stage is a time of fundamental changes in rural structure when industrialization and urbanization are further expanded. Large-scale migration of the rural population is in progress and both labor costs and rural property values are steeply rising. Long term capital investments become attractive —interest in short term agricultural projects wane. Investment in farmland is more likely to be a consolidation of farmland. Grain production has a greater demand for land concentration than that of other crops. Specialization and modernization in agricultural production can be expected in the effort to increase efficiency and production and remain competitive.

Large-scale farming operations go through these three stages and look and behave differently in each. Agricultural development in China proceeds hand in hand with the process of national industrialization. These last two stages mark a reversal in roles from agricultural supplementing industry to industry beginning to supplement agriculture. But all three of these stages will be seen to co-exist in different places in China and in view of this we should never seek to impose an indiscriminate "uniformity" on all areas throughout the nation. Rather, we should be flexible enough to make decisions based on the actual situations prevailing in different places.

China's large-scale farming should adopt the most efficient forms while respecting the preferences of the vast number of farmers.

1) Large-scale production develops via the sale and consolidation of farmland. Increased production is usually accomplished by specialized "families" or associations, such as grain-producing families, vegetable-growing families, etc.

2) There are also "corporation farming" families.

3) Communities and farmers have special relationships. Farmers grow the crops in the fields. Through taxes and funds they support their communities. At the same time, communities, which have various degrees of economic power based on their skill in management and the support they have received from enterprises, may assist the farmers by establishing public works and services such as water, roads, telecommunication and transportation.

4) There are shareholding cooperatives.

5) Cooperative farms differ from the past collective cooperatives in that they have funds to invest and are able to cover their basic expenses. They are also in control of the efficiency of their operation, can reduce superfluous manpower in the fields and have more responsibility for the prosperity of the enterprise.

F. Bringing About Universal Property Right Reform Using the Breakthroughs in Farmland Property Right Reform as a Model

The development of township-run enterprises should be along the lines of a shareholding system or shareholding cooperative system which must clarify property right relationships and change the earlier system of operation.

The ambiguity of property right relationships continues to restrict the development of township-run enterprises. In theory, the assets of these enterprises belong to all the members of the community, but in fact, the ambiguity of these property rights creates the same problems as exist in the state-owned enterprises. These township-run enterprises were usually run directly by administrative arms at town and village levels, and they are still very much restricted by local administrations. There is no clear-cut line separating these enterprises and the government administrations over them. It is usual that each will do business on behalf of the other and it is common at village and town levels for the administration to consider the profits of these enterprises as their private reserves and withdraw such at will with insufficient regard to the enterprise's optimum development.

One important approach to the resolution of these problems is to reorganize the property right system of township-run enterprises into a shareholding or shareholding cooperative system. For example, by allowing farmers to buy shares with their farmland, investment funds, injected technology or even with their labor, property rights of township-run enteprises will become clarified and form a driving force for further development.

By dividing all or part of the collective assets into shares on the basis of "to each according to his work and to each according to his investment" each household could receive dividends. In addition, other methods of raising funds or attracting foreign investments may be employed to expand the capital of the enterprises or even start shareholding companies which will further increase farmers' income.

It is essential to encourage the pioneer spirit in these township-run enterprises and to support them so that the superiority of this system is demonstrated and promoted broadly.

The efficiency of large-scale operations can be realized through such groups. Township-run enterprises which have produced agricultural raw materials as their base, under the right conditions, could cooperate with the processing, storage, transportation and marketing industries making production, supply and marketing a coordinated process. We are talking about an economy with various organizational forms. And finding and establishing the most optimum forms might require experiment. Nevertheless, it is necessary to push for inter-regional large-scale development of township-run enterprises.

Such large-scale development manifests primarily from regional division of work and organization. If efficient and based on existing conditions such guidance is conducive of bringing about collective efficiency and avoiding wastes of energy and land resources.

Small industrial areas can be established with towns or cities as the center. Factories and workshops can be built and gotten into production. Meanwhile mortgage loans can be used to initiate infrastructure construction, such loans guaranteed by future lease of land.

We must speed up the process of establishing shareholding credit cooperatives and simultaneously clarify and codify the financial property right relationships in the rural cooperative system.

At present, credit cooperatives are economic entities that nominally operate independently and hold responsibilities for their profits and losses. But at the same time they are factually subsidiaries of the Agricultural Bank which is entrusted by the People's Bank of China to run these cooperatives on its behalf. Credit cooperatives carry a heavy workload of providing loans and overseeing actual business operations. The Agricultural Bank occasionally uses funds from these cooperatives to make up for shortages. Hence, credit cooperatives could hardly operate independently. After going back and forth several times from "nongovernmental" to "official," these credit cooperatives have an ambiguous relationship in regards to the rights of their own assets. And consequently the percentage of share capital from farmers is not high. Now it is imperative to clarify and codify this property right relationship. Through the establishment of a shareholding system and by selling shares to further disconnect such cooperatives from adminstrative agencies we can turn such cooperatives into vital commercial and financial organizations.

III. We Must Perfect Macro-Adjustment with the Aim of Establishing Agricultural Produce Markets

A. We Must Learn to Accurately Estimate the Actual Situations of Supply and Demand and Err Neither in the Direction of Pessimism Nor Optimism

The problems of agriculture, farmers and the countryside have become front-page concerns of the whole society. The most pressing ones are whether the supply and demand of agricultural by-products can be stabilized by the market and whether the rising food prices can be checked.

Here are four reasons to avoid too pessimistic an estimate of the current situation of agricultural supply and demand.

First. For the moment, Chinese farmers have no big problems in producing and consuming their own produce as well as the by-products. Farmers in less developed areas have enough to eat and eat better food than in the past. Farmers in developed areas have sufficient food and nutrition. Only farmers in disaster and poverty-stricken areas are besieged with food problems, but this poses no threat to the overall economy and more than 80 percent of China's population have a reliable supply of food.

Second. For residents of small towns and cities this is also not a serious problem. As these markets cover only a small area, the prices can adjust by both the amount of production and the need of consumption—and any shortage is easy to resolve.

Third. In medium-sized and large cities there are well developed markets. The supply and need of high quality food is good and well adjusted by price and so there is no crisis at all. Any shortage is adjusted rapidly as the price increases and the demand reduces.

Fourth. In the past two years there were two areas (both in

medium- and-large sized cities) where a balance of supply and demand was hard to maintain. One was in the food products comsumed by low-income residents and the other was the raw materials needed to maintain minimum production by inefficient state-owned enterprises engaged in light indutry. Thus we can see that any supply "crisis" in the past few years was by no means universal, but limited, and periodic. And in both cases boiled down to a lack of purchasing power—of both the residents and enterprises concerned—to purchase the materials they needed at market prices.

The emphasis of current agricultural policy is almost entirely concentrated on increasing the effective supply of products. If the crux at present—the insufficient demand for some products—is ignored, the supply of cotton and grain will not be stimulated.

As the core of the problem is the low-income population and low-efficiency enterprises in cities the problem can be solved not by generally giving financial subsidies to urban dwellers for their food consumption but by fully concentrating the limited finances available to ensure these low-income earners have both enough to eat and enough to wear.

The central government cannot be relied upon to resolve the problem of food supply for urban low-income makers and raw material supply for the class of light-industrial enterprises described above. In the first place it is the local governments' strong point to identify low-income makers and to organize flexible adjustment. Therefore it must be a long-term policy to delegate more responsibility to local government in balancing the market.

It is important to ban inter-regional restrictions on the trade of grain and other products and to stop any action that would impose mandatory purchases of goods at low prices. With these bans in force there will be no big disturbances in the countryside.

Localities may, under supervision, adopt different measures to solve the problem of instability of produce supply and need. For example, in the interests of opening up markets, appropriate subsidies can be given to urban low-income workers, or some provinces may wish to try increasing the agricultural tax to 10 percent but then abandon the collection of all other fees and charges.

In the meantime, it is important to accelerate the reform of the following three kinds of state-owned enterprises:

a) Inefficient and loss-producing companies that utilize agricultural produce for their raw materials must either be allowed to declare bankruptcy or be reorganized to ensure that such agricultural products are going only to high-efficiency enterprises. b) Efforts must be made to increase efficiency and strengthen the management of those industries which produce agricultural equipment. The cost of their products must also be reduced, and profits increased. c) State-owned enterprises selling grain and food must also accelerate reform. It is important to break the monopoly now prevailing in this industry. Those agencies which link farmers with their markets must also be made to operate competitively.

B. A Problem Has Emerged Whereby Current Means of Macro-Adjustment Do Not Conform to the Market System

The rural economic reform of the 90s saw the start of the breaking down of arbitrary divisions between industry and agriculture and between cities and countryside. Studies have proven that rural reform has been closely linked with urban reform. For example, farmers in the millions have come to work in cities; farmers in the millions are doing business in the vegetables and other agricultural products markets in cities; farmers have contracted business in cities and have started to build their small towns.

The key to rural economic reform lies in the complete freeing up of prices for agricultural products including those of grain and cotton. But this in turn requires the acceleration of the full realization and bringing into being of market mechanics. But this problem impacts not only on the countryside but on urban interests as well. The conflicts between urban and rural interests that were caused by the purchase and sale of cotton and grain in the past two years became very acute in some areas. To handle shortages governments forced farmers to plant more grain. This resulted in grain being purchased at lower prices when there was a bumper harvest. Can farmers be blamed for taking self-protective actions such as reducing agricultural investments or diversifying into non-agricultural business in order to guarantee higher and more secure incomes?

Though government has decided that product prices must be kept free in the open market, whenever a conflict between urban and rural interests arises and the government fails to balance these interests, it inevitably resorts to old policies which hurt the direct interests of the farmers.

There are two extreme cases that deserve study. Neither is beneficial.

In the first scenario, all the products are dumped onto the market while the government stands by and provides no guidance or structure. Agriculture has its own special features. Spontaneous operations of the market are not capable of completely caring for agricultural interests. Agricultural production is periodic, and relying only on the market can result in a difficult life for farmers and adversely effect the development of the national economy and social stability. A "spontaneous market" price mechanism can be just as detrimental to agriculture and the farmers' interest as the old traditional price system of planned economy.

The second case is the return of the outmoded adjustment measures of the traditional planned economy in the name of macro-adjustment. Such mechanisms include dumping surplus commodities on the market when supply exceeds demand. This has the dual effect of lower prices making it hard to sell grain and cotton. When supply is inadequate to meet demand a situation arises in which grain and cotton are scarce until adequate supplies can be obtained through extra labor and compulsory measures.

At this time of transforming to a market system the questions that still must be resolved are: how to coordinate the relationships between rural and urban interests and those between the state and farmers, how to make macro-adjustment policy more practical and economic measures more workable, and how to gradually reduce and finally abandon the old methods of administrative intervention of the planned economy and replace them with new measures in line with the laws of the market economy.

C. The Drastic Fluctuations in Both the Products Prices and the Price Policies Over the Past Two Years Show That Current Macro-Adjustment Measures Are out of Synch with the Establishment of Rural Markets

Freeing up grain prices is the key to the establishment of a stable agricultural products market. The government immediately intervened when grain prices started to rise after the autumn harvest of 1993. But farmers were very dissatisfied with the administrative measures. The way to incorporate a degree of macroeconomic control in an efficient manner within the framework of a market system is a question for further study.

D. In the Process of Pushing Forward the Establishment of a Commodities Market, It Is Essential to Establish a Corresponding Standard Macroeconomic System Which Is Able to Adjust the Rural Market Economy

Financial policy must be used to ensure an increase in fundamental agricultural investment. a. The increase of production and guarantee of balanced supply are the fundamental measures needed to stabilize products markets. In the past two years, the central government's agricultural investment was not carried out satisfactorily. The national financial budget for agricultural investment in 1994 totaled 52.3 billion yuan, about 9.63 percent of the total financial expenditure, a 15 percent increase over the previous year. But by September of that year less than 50 percent of the year's planned agricultural budget had been expended. Quite some local governments cut down the percentage of agricultural investment. b. Another important goal of financial policy is the establishment of two separate funds of financial reserves. One can be used to adjust the volume of important commodities into or out of the market (thus stabilizing the market). The other is to deal with natural disasters, wars and accidents. c. Financial policy must be coordinated with price policy, industrial policy and foreign trade policy, to give fixed subsidies to agricultural products to protect agriculture, to stabilize prices, encourage export, etc.

Taxation policy must be applied so as to strengthen the protection of agriculture and farmers as well as reducing farmers' burdens. a. In recent years, agricultural taxes have become too heavy. More and more fund collections have been added exceeding 20 percent of a farmer's income. It is necessary to reform agricultural taxation and to discard unreasonable fees and charges including those hidden under "other names." b. The determination of an agricultural tax rate should proceed from the principle that it must be conducive to the development of a weak agriculturural sector and must protect the farmers income in the market economy. Therefore the tax rate can neither be too high nor increase too fast—rather, agricultural taxes should be reduced or waived appropriately if necessary. In 1994 after tax system reform, taxation on township-run enterprises increased sharply with an increasing taxation categories. In the first five months of 1994, the total taxation on township-run enterprises increased by 35 percent over that of the same period in the previous year, about 5.8 percent higher than the national tax increase in same period. The loss of 9 percent by township-run enterprises increased to 16 percent from January to June of 1994. It is clear that taxes on township-run enterprises should be lowered to promote their further development.

It is necessary to establish a sound rural financial system and use financial policies to guarantee the investment of agricultural loans and credits. a. The system must coordinate the work of policy banks, commercial banks and cooperative financial organizations, to ensure agricultural loans and credit investments, to revitalize rural financial business, and to increase the flow of rural finance into the rural economy. b. Great efforts should be made to develop rural financial market, through which, the distribution of rural fund, technology and manpower are adjusted and rural resources are properly arranged. c. After the restructuring the rural financial system, the Agricultural Bank and the Rural Cooperative Bank can operate entirely in accord with usual commercial principles to channel loans to regions and industries

117

with a high level of efficiency. That is why the state should stipulate the scope and ratio of agricultural loans that rural commercial banks may provide specifically in terms of interest subsidies. In the meantime, the state should plan a certain percentage of the annual currency to be used for a special purpose to the Rural Cooperative Bank for its further distribution in the form of agricultural production loans. Rural financial agencies which invest in rural financial operations should be rewarded with low tax or even tax-free policy.

Price policy should be applied properly and prices of agricultural products should be stabilized through a stable production. a. Target prices or minimum protective prices should be fixed to guide commodity market price. This has the effect of both stimulating the production of major agricultural products and upgrading the farmers' income level. b. It is necessary to develop agricultural commodity futures markets, to establish the long-term pricing mechanism and ensure the stable production and sale of these products.

It is necessary to apply import and export trade policy to adjust the supply and demand of domestic agricultural products markets. a. China's agricultural products markets should attach importance to their connection with international markets, as such connection can be the source of the greatest gains. b. The state should make full use of import and export trade to adjust the supply and need of domestic commodities markets.

E. It Is Important to Implement a Protective Policy on Agriculture, But from a Long-Term Point of View, Importance Should Be Attached to Avoiding Excessive Protection

Under market economy, agriculture is a weak industry which, because of its high social effects and low efficiency, needs to be protected to some extent for better development. China's agriculture has a relative weak foundation, so its development needs more policy support from the state.

At present the major problem in the rural economic development is the protection of agriculture, but from a long-term consideration, it is necessary to attach importance to avoiding excessive protection of agriculture. Over-protection of agriculture may lead to a series of unfavorable consequences. First, about 80 percent of China's population is in agriculture, so as a matter of fact, it is difficult to implement a policy of the minority protecting the majority, moreover, the state does not have such financial power. Secondly, it would stimulate a high-cost mode of production, neither conducive to intensive agricultural management nor favorable to the optimum utilization of agricultural resources. Thirdly, it would cause over-production of agricultural products. If the government tries to absorb all overproduction it will fail because it is beyond the government's financial ability. But if the government does nothing there will be outstanding debt. Farmers will suffer greater losses. Fourthly, it won't be conducive to linking China's domestic commodity markets with international markets.

And ultimately, no matter how much effort may be expended in protecting agricultural markets, the final resolution lies in bringing up the efficiency of the agriculture so as to increase its competitiveness in a market economy.

F. Push Forward Both the Industrialization of the Rural Economy and the Acceleration of the Reform of China's Traditional Agricultural System

It is necessary to adopt various kinds of measures suiting local conditions. a. By taking advantage of local resources a village can develop its own products or industry to generate quality products for large-scale production. b. Measures can be taken by the market such as increasing specialized production by developing commodities markets, particularly specialized wholesale markets. c. Measures can be instituted by leading enterprises to integrate production, processing and sales businesses with a single industry or product. Such enterprises as processing, fridge-storage and transportation enterprises should take a leading role. d. To meet the needs of the market, trans-regional management for agricultural products may be adopted and the role of processing enterprises should be brought into full play. The key to industrializing the rural economy lies in doing a good job of establishing leading enterprises and supporting a group of leading enterprises that have a strong driving power.

G. Place Further Emphasis on Developing Commodities Markets and Other Related Markets Including Futures Markets

1) Put the emphasis on developing farmland, fund, labor and technology markets.

The rural market system is incomplete if there are only commodities markets without ancillary markets. The goal of establishing a farmland market is to give farmers relatively complete right to use the farmland, to solve the problems of the circulation, lease, mortgage and inheritance of farmland. It will also enable some farmers to leave farmland and enter into non-agricultural industry. Establishing rural cooperative funds is an effective way to develop financial markets and widen new channels for fund-raising. The development of rural technological market can accelerate the transformation of scientific and technological achievements in their application to agriculture. A labor market is conducive to bridging regional gaps and solving the problem of farmers' low income. It is estimated that in recent years there have been 6 million people migrated from Sichuan Province every year. If on the average each worker remitted 1000 yuan back to Sichuan every year, the total remittance would reach 6 billion yuan, more than the annual fund that the government has earmarked to support the development of township-run enterprises in mid-west China. Moreover, these migrating workers would bring back to their homes technology, market information and experience in modern production. They are the backbone in developing rural economy in the rural areas of mid-west China.

2) Let's boldly experiment with commodities futures markets.

China's commodities futures market is at an initial stage. In order to bring into full play the guiding role of commodities prices in futures markets, it is necessary to allow major agricultural products to enter into futures markets such as rice, wheat and cotton.

In the meantime, it is important to construct a sound management system and to work out regulations and laws governing the operation of such a futures market. The market must be managed in strict accordance with these laws and importance must be placed on self-restraint in futures and the standardization of organizational forms of futures exchanges.

IV. Promoting Coordinated Development Between the Urban and Rural in Advancing the Establishment of Rural Markets

A. Let the Establishment of Rural Markets Lead Urban Markets to Promote Coordinated Development Between the Rural and the Urban

Under the traditional planned economic system, the state macro-adjustment tended favor urban interests at the expense of rural. Along with the all-round development of economic reform, the conflicts between the urban and the rural has been greatly alleviated. But practices in past two years have shown that deeper problems in urban-rural relations have not been fundamentally solved.

Importance should be attached to the following issues promoting a coordinated urban-rural development. a. It is necessary to establish commodity and essential factors of production markets that link the rural and urban sectors and promote the effective combination and reasonable circulation of capital, labor, land, technology, etc. b. It is important to reform the current residence registration system, to establish a nationwide unified identification of residence registration system and to allow surplus rural laborers to work in cities via labor markets. c. Rural industrial structure should be optimized. At the time of developing the first industry in a rural area, it is important to encourage and support the development of rural processing industries that effectively use agricultural and other rural resources. The development of township-run enterprises should be guided in such a way as to permit the unique advantages of the rural and urban industrial structures to supplement each other. d. Construction of rural towns can also be stepped up to create conditions that allow integration of the urban and rural economies.

B. In the Process of Accelerating the Establishment of Rural Markets, It Is Necessary to Support and Protect the Weak Agricultural Areas and Promote a Coordinated and Sustained Development of Industry and Agriculture

Under a market economy, agriculture needs support and protection from the government. But this is not only a need of the agriculture itself but a requirement of industry and the national economy as a whole.

C. It Is Vital to Accelerate the Establishment of Rural Markets and the Creation of Balanced Regional Products Relations That Suit the Market Economy

The importance of regional balance of major agricultural products has long been accented in state planned allocations. But since the rural economic reform, the old relationship of regional balance has not been changed. Instead there have been clashes and breakdowns of the old system in various regions under market economy. The drastic fluctuations of agricultural product prices in 1993 and 1994 had been largely attributed to regional conflicts and breakdowns in traditional balanced regional relations.

The development of regional economies is seriously imbalanced in China and the regional imbalances of agricultural products development is more serious still. This sharp difference of regional development cannot be expected to be entirely solved by the regions themselves. The establishment of a unified nationwide market and the formation of a nationally unified market mechanism have to be quickened. At the time when we preach governors' or mayors' responsibility for the supply of vegetables and grain, it is highly necessary to attach importance to a national solution of regional balance of agricultural products. The establishment of rural markets requires to break the traditional balanced relationship of regional agricultural products, break through regional blockades, get rid of regional protectionism and establish a national unified intact market so as to lay down a market foundation for establishing macro adjustment mechanism.

In recent years, China's rural economy saw increasingly larger gaps between various regions. One province or autonomous region's rural economic power might double another's. Unbalanced regional development will hinder not only the further development of rural economy but social stability as well. Two aspects of rural regional economic development deserve attention. One is to bring into full play the comparative advantages of rural resources and production factors in different areas and develop agriculture enterprises with comparatively high efficiency. The other is that the state should give necessary support to less developed areas.

D. Since the Key to the Development of Small Towns Lies in Farmers' Enthusiasm in Building Small Towns This Enthusiasm Must Be Generated and Then Protected

Emerging small towns and cities in the countryside are not only the base for the development of rural industry but also a groundwork for the transition of the rural society. In the past ten years, small towns and cities have become centers of production, services, entertainment, education and information for farmers. The diversified social functions of small towns met farmers' increasing needs in many different ways. And they began to rely on these small towns and cities.

Longgang Town of Zhejiang Province, a small town built with funds raised by farmers, has developed into a town with a population of 130,000 people and an output value of 800 million yuan.

The main approach taken to transform villages into towns should be that of promoting the growth of industry.

The township-run and family-run enterprises in China are scattered in "every village or household." This kind of layout has shortcomings such as inconvenient transportation, less-informed, wasteful utilization of farmland resources and added expenses in trade. Industrial concentration can remedy all of these and is conducive to acquiring external interests while at the same time lessening restrictions on communal interests. This helps rural industry to modernize on a par with that of the cities. Central towns and cities should be chosen as the centers for rural industry and local governments should actively improve the investment environment of these towns or cities and formulate corresponding policies to encourage township-run or family-run enterprises to move into these towns or cities.

It is time to take advantage of the rising trend of new economic development zones that we have witnessed in recent years. Such zones can lead the way in building new types of small cities or towns for industrial development, trade and tourism.

Farmers' enthusiasm should be mobilized to speed up the construction of small industrial zones, development zones, trade zones and township-run enterprise centers. On the basis of the chained development of township-run industries, new types of small towns or cities will be built by strengthening the construction of infrastructure.

Tertiary industry should be given a leading role in the construction of small towns or cities. For instance, border towns should be built by taking advantage of geographical location and specialized production, developing border trade and local trade. Specialized markets and grand-sized trade markets can be set up. The traditional village free markets should be expanded and reformed.

Township-run enterprises should be encouraged and assisted in the construction of small towns and cities in joint-ownership or inter-regional incorporation with other urban enterprises or foreign enterprises.

E. Stable Establishment of Rural Markets Requires a Streamlining of Administrative Structure at County Level

Since the county is where urban and rural meet and macro and micro join together, the comprehensive reform at county level bears special significance to the development of rural economy. At present, the increasingly bigger administrative organizations at county level have become a heavy burden on rural economic development as they are too expensive to be supported in many counties. Thus, the first step for the comprehensive reform at county level is to restructure and change their functions.

It is necessary to establish service networks in agricultural machinery, water conservation, science and technology, production methods and others at county and village levels. Such should aim at big markets and high efficiency. In the meantime, the construction of accounting, auditing, legal counseling, notary, information and intermediary agencies should be intensified and the relations among governments, markets and farmers be smoothed.

The solution to agricultural investment rests largely on county financial institutions. Banks, credit cooperatives and insurance companies should help farmers raise funds through various channels and provide insurance services. They should also give policy support to rural cooperative funds and work to provide financial services to the collectives.

F. A Pressing Task in Coordinating Urban-Rural Relations Is to Productively Channel Redundant Rural Manpower in an Orderly Manner

Surplus agricultural manpower is increasing. Migration is on the rise and this trend will continue. So scientific judgement must be made to channel this flow so as to reduce the pressure on and maintain the social stability and order in cities.

It is estimated that China currently has 100 to 120 million surplus rural laborers and in the years to come we will see an annual increase of 6 to 7 million. Agricultural modernization and large scale production in the countryside will release a large quantities of unskilled labor power from their old jobs while these same technological advancements in township-run enterprises will reduce the number of new jobs available to supernumerary rural laborers. From 1984 to 1988, township-run enterprises created 63.11 million new jobs with an annual increase of 12.62

million jobs. This amounts to 117.4 percent of the annual increase of rural manpower over the same period. From 1989 to 1993, they created 19.11 million new jobs with an annual increase of 3.82 million, about 45.6 percent of the increase of manpower of the same period in the countryside.

In coming years, the "flow of migrating workers" will continue to expand. The rural redundant laborers will be circulating faster between cities and the countryside, bringing impact and social risks to big and medium-sized cities.

Strict "work permit" requirements tend to lead to regional blockades. Migratory workers should either be digested in the countryside or channelled into specific towns and cities where they can be utilized.

China's big cities cannot bear the continuous buffetting of this "flow of migrating workers." Social stability and city order can only be maintained through the ordered channelling of this flow. Some places adopted "blockade" tactics by issuing "work permits." Studies showed, however, that this led to corruption and lease-finding actions, unfavorable to the formation of a unified labor market.

Small cities and towns are the first "reservoirs" for the rural surplus laborers who leave their farmland. Most of these laborers will be held in the small towns and cities which will expand into bigger cities by absorbing these migrating workers. So, the development of small towns and cities should be taken as a "diverting project" to alleviate unemployment pressures in the present and for a period of time in the future.

Big and medium-sized cities should provide more job opportunities for farmers who have just come to cities to be engaged in tertiary industry.

The immediate goal of residence registration system reform should be the gradual loosening of residence registration restrictions in county seats. All the farmers who have a fixed job, income and residence in a county seat should be allowed to settle down there and be entitled to the same rights and obligations as same as the local urban residents.

The residence registration restrictions in small cities should also be appropriately reduced. Farmers who have fixed jobs, income and residence in cities should be allowed to have residence there after paying a certain amount in city construction fees.

Farmers who have been residing in big cities for some years and have a stable job, income and housing shall be given "blue-seal residence certificate." Those who hold "blue-seal residence certificate" are entitled to the same treatment as the urban residents in employment, application for a vendor's counter and industrial and business licenses, as well as the day-care and schooling of their children.

V. The Promotion of the Establishment of Rural Markets and the Change of Government Functions

A. It Is an Important Obligation of the Government to Educate and Train Peasants

The low educational level of agricultural workers in China seriously impedes the transfer of agricultural scientific and technological achievements and the improvement of productivity. According to estimates by agricultural specialists from the United Nations and the United States, only one sixth of the increase of agricultural products comes from the expansion of cultivated land in the coming decade. The rest will come from the biological technical revolution. Since 1957, China's total arable land has been shrinking each year, and the total arable land cannot be expanded in the years to come because reclaimable farmland resources are themselves becoming exhausted. The only approach to increasing total output of grain in China comes from increasing the average yield per hectare. And this relies on scientific and technological achievements and their popularization and transfer. It is calculated that the contribution of technical advancement to the increase of the total agricultural production value accounted only 28 percent in the Seventh Five-Year Plan period (1986-1990), seven percent less than that in the Sixth Five-Year Plan period.

The reason why science and technology has made so small a contribution to China's agricultural development is closely linked with the low quality of the education of agricultural laborers. Of the 340 million agricultural workers, 25 percent are illiterate or semi-illiterate. And 38.4 percent graduated from primary school while less than 29.4 percent of them finished junior middle school. After the liberation in 1949, 1.5 million agricultural technicians were trained in vocational middle schools and above, but now no more than 150,000 of these are still working in agriculture.

The low-level education of agricultural workers can not meet the need of China's agricultural modernization, nor can it meet the need of rural economic markets. This has become a striking block to China's agricultural development. The key to the resolution of the problem lies in overhauling the education and training of farmers, particularly in popularizing compulsory education in the countryside, eliminating illiteracy and making vocational education and scientific and technological training easily accessible.

Agricultural training should be adopted as an important function by the government. Government agencies should play a leading role in providing such training. Organizing various vocational education programs and training institutions for farmers should be an important task of the government. Such programs must be carried out through various channels. China has over 800 million farmers, and training them presents the largest and most complex educational problem that the country faces. To this we must add the shortage of education expenditures. This calls for multi-channel, multi-grade and all-round agricultural training. The institutions to popularize agricultural science and technology may be changed into an agricultural training system. Through efforts in the past 40 years, an agricultural science and technology popularization network at county, town and village levels has been established. The network can be further improved and given new functions such as educating and training farmers.

B. We Must Use the Legal System to Reassure Farmers of Their Rights by Ensuring That the Legal System Actually Does Accomplish This

1) Social stability and the expectations of farmers in the current economic transition period is related to the fundamental smooth operation and overall security of the economy. It is necessary to attach great importance to this.

The farmers expect relative stability and such expectations need guarantee through legislation and from the legal system. Without some basic legislation, farmers are always worried about possible arbitrary changes of policy—this dampens their enthusiasm for long-term investment and production. In the transitional period, what farmers' expect in terms of future changes in the social economy will continue to have great impact on their economic actions, so particular attention should be attached to calming them down on this point. Strengthening legislation and enforcing existing legal guarantees are important measures to stabilize the farmers and the countryside.

2) The countryside needs laws that all must obey. These laws should regulate the reforms already achieved and should be standardized. Effective policy must exist to stabilize the countryside and guarantee the gains already made. At present the key is to formulate some basic laws and decrees which embody the progress of the rural reform so far and guarantees the framework and guidelines for operating in a rural market economic system.

It is necessary to work out regulations regarding the management of contracting farmland. It is necessary to confirm farmers' long-term rights to use farmland and clearly define and protect these long-term rights and interests by legislation. It is necessary to place some conditions on the circulating relationship in contracting farming, and to standardize the farmland circulation market, to clearly define the relationship between the collective and farmers and that between the state and farmers. In short all actions by the state and farmers must be standardized.

It is equally necessary to formulate laws and regulations relating to agricultural investment, macro-adjustment, resources protection, science and technology investment and popularization, market establishment, intermediary agencies in the countryside, etc., so that the rural reform and agricultural development has rules to follow.

3) Legal construction in the countryside may start its experiment at village level.

Rural legal construction under a market economy is quite a complicated matter in many respects, and may need a long period of experimentation before it can be fully implemented. At present, experimentation can begin in villages. Later, after adequate experience and successful trials, these experiments can be initiated throughout the entire nation.

4) Management should be conducted in accordance with law by applying the method of contractual agreement.

Some areas that will find contractual management suitable include: reducing farmers' burdens, family planning, contracted production. In such cases the prefectural agricultural commission, family planning commission, prefectural court and other competent departments should jointly work out letters of contract which will be signed by village committees and farmers and notarized by notary offices. The farmers, village committee and department concerned each keeps a copy of the contract. Once it is signed, the contract will be legally binding and each side will be held legally accountable in case it is violated.

Chapter IV
Regional Economic Development
in the Transition of China's Economy

China's reform and opening policy is a progressive solution to national conditions which were gravely out of balance. The first state actions called for the support and development of the south-eastern coastal regions, which once they had provided themselves with better conditions would be able to push the development of the central and western areas. It can be said that this reform policy has had great success. The rapid development of the eastern coastal regions in South China and other parts has speeded up the development of the Yangtze River valley, thus laying the foundation and pre-requisite to the further development of western China. China is a big country, and has historically seen an unbalanced rate of development among its different areas. This problem can by no means be fully solved within a short period. So it is not enough to look at present "gaps in regional economic and social development." We must at the same time adopt practical reform and opening policies that will be favorable to the medium and long term development of all regional economies.

I. Regional Common Development and Economic Integration

A. Regional Common Development Is the Main Problem for China's Further Development

Inconsistencies in China's regional development has become a national phenomenon and an obstacle to economic integration and the overall development of the society. Therefore, the problem of regional common development should be given a lot of importance.

Since the carrying out of the reform and opening policy, regional gaps, particulary that between the coastal regions and the interior, have continued to widen. Taking the average GDP per capita as an index, there was a difference of 2,332 yuan in average GDP per capita between Shanghai and Guizhou in 1978 and it increased to 5,785 yuan in 1991; while the difference of the average GDP per capita between Shanghai and Guangdong was 2,131 yuan in 1978, and it was increased to 3,852 yuan in 1991.

At the same time, the widening of the income gap of residents in different regions is different in range and has become even greater. Looking at the income of peasants, the average net income per capita of those peasants in eastern coastal regions where they are provided with advantageous geographical conditions and a better economic foundation, reached 1,221 yuan in 1993, an increase of 21.8 percent over the previous year and a rise of 11.1 percentage points in the range of growth. Among the six provinces and the municipality directly under the Central Government where the growth of the average net income per capita exceeded 20 percent, five are situated in the eastern area, namely Shanghai, Zhejiang, Fujian, Guangdong and Guangxi. The average net income per capita of peasants in the central area was 802 yuan, an increase of 15.4 percent over the previous year and a rise of 2.7 percentage points in the range of growth; all but two of these were in the 10-20 percent range with Anhui exceeding 20 percent and Heilongjiang lower than 10 percent. The average income per capita of peasants in the western area was 611 yuan, increasing 9.3 percent over the previous year with the range of growth remaining the same: among these the growth ranges of Yunnan, Ningxia and Xinjiang were below 10 percent.

There also exist obvious differences in the income levels of city residents. According to the statistics, the 1993 average income per capita of residents in the eastern, central and western areas were respectively 2,878 yuan, 1,886.8 yuan and 2,045.1 yuan, increasing 31.9, 24.9 and 22.4 percent over the previous year. Both the per capita average of absolute income and range of growth for residents in the central and western areas were lower than the national average level.

B. A Scientific Analysis on the Unbalanced Development and the Main Contradictions of the Near Future Should Be Made

We should scientifically analyze the present unequal situation but while recognizing the true contradictions should not exaggerate the problem.

Since 1978, China has adjusted its regional reform policy. The emphasis has been shifted from inland construction to investment of coastal areas where economic benefits are higher. In the efforts to achieve these benefits large amounts of capital, talented personnel, and other production elements flooded into the southeastern coastal regions. This greatly strengthened the economic vitality and growth of those regions. This growth first of all led to the development of the entire coastal area which supports almost half of China's population, but at the same time it has also, to a certain extent, sparked the development of the central and western areas as well, promoting the Chinese economy as a whole.

Owing to the rapid economic growth achieved in this area over the last few years, and supported by the unique conditions of its geography, resources, climate, humanism and history, we can expect to continue to see part of the capital seeking high returns to flow into the south-eastern coastal regions. The reality is that this so-called "unbalanced regional development" is an existing condition and will be further extended. It can even be said that this is an inevitable consequence at a certain state of reform and opening.

Our target is to work towards common development in the midst of this situation and gradually secure the change from "common development" to "balanced development." To solve this problem, the difficulty is how to handle the relationship between "efficiency and equity" and between "short term and long term."

China must continue to develop its overall economy and

maintain its rapid growth. But at the same time, in regional economic development, we must place priority on increasing efficiency by making the best use of limited production resources for economic development of specific regions. Regional equity must be taken into consideration while at the same time superior regions must still be given priority of resources so as to gain a better economic return. At the same time, financial support for the main industries and departments of relatively backward regions should be given to reinforce and encourage these areas to work towards self development. In this way, it will create an overall economic upsurge within the framework of a rational pattern of unbalanced development.

C. Regional Economic Development Must Be Promoted in Line with the Principles of Market Economy

Regional integration lowers costs and the formation of urban centers is an effective way to build markets.

It is obvious that if the products of a region could be consumed in that region there would be a vast savings in transportation and other costs. When external competition can be changed to internal coordination, competitive expenses can be enormously reduced. Hence what we call "regional integration" will generate greater productive force.

The way for common development is to build urban centers in those regions, like those of the Yangtze River Delta, the Zhujiang River Delta and that around the Bohai district. The traditional division of administrative areas has obstructed the effective development of coordination, while the building of a socialist system of market economy urgently demands the establishment of a unified market. The economic significance of the construction of urban areas is to promote the formation of common and unified markets among different regions.

The key to this regional integration is the creation of a strong enterprise system and optimization of competitive mechanism. This means to remove all market barriers so that market resources can be jointly enjoyed. To optimize the competitive environment, regional competition must be reduced while that amongst enterprises is intensified.

Judging from historical experience, a country will usually exhibit a polarization effect in its initial stages of economic development, and then after a certain period of accumulation of international commodities, capital investments, and foreign techniques, it will begin to manifest a process of proliferation. At this time it will not only extend its export of commodities to foreign countries, but gradually transfer its own industries, capital and techniques to foreign countries. If China expects to occupy an advantageous position during the course of the 4th and 5th long cycles of world economy, it ought to shorten its process of polarization as much as possible. This can be done by alternating polarization and proliferation.

China's economic structure is pluralistic: it has both vast but economically backward rural areas and relatively economically developed eastern coastal areas; it not only possesses industries provided with lower-level labour and concentrated capital, but also industries with advanced technology and concentrated learning. Therefore, it is practically possible for China to carry out simultaneously processes of polarization and proliferation.

Administrative measures should be avoided in promoting the development of a regional economy. During the transition of China's economy all must be done in line with the principle of market economy. For instance, in order to strengthen macroregulation by the Central Government we have to establish a unified market (or regional common market). This benefits the regions involved and also strengthens the market system.

II. Transition from Unbalanced Development to Balanced Development

A. We Must Pay Attention to the Study and Resolution of the Question of Transition from Unbalanced Development to Balanced Development

As we have mentioned above, the widening gap in per capita income in the economic development of different regions is a phenomenon that cannot be entirely avoided in the process of transition. In such a big country as China, such gaps cannot help but lead to some social problems. The large scale migrations of the labor force (about 80 million people annually and increasing every year) exacerbate this. Therefore reducing this gap is a matter of importance. If it cannot be entirely eliminated it can at least be kept under control.

B. We Must Correctly Judge the Influence of Foreign Investment on China's Regional Economy

To promote the liberalization of trade and investment and to realize common prosperity are the targets of the joint effort of countries in the Asian-Pacific area. The participation of foreign investment has become an important factor affecting both China's regional economies and her macro-economy as well.

The opening of regions is the jumping off point in China's strategy of opening to the outside world. This uses international economic strength to enhance the growth of the domestic economy and upgrade China's industrial structure and includes the absorbing of direct foreign investment, establishing foreign enterprises and channelling China's national economic forces into the international economic system. Foreign capitals are invariably seeking profitable sites for investment. Many countries, including the developed countries, are trying to attract foreign investments in a thousand and one ways. The continued high speed growth of China's economy has provided excellent opportunities for foreign investment in the face of an international trend of recession. The most favored, of course, has been the south-eastern coastal regions where the climate, geographical location and preferential policy have created good conditions for the inflow of large quantities of foreign capital. The concentration of foreign investment in this area, of course, is what has caused the unbalanced economic development. It has brought both rewards and problems, and this conflict deserves our serious study so it can be resolved.

C. We Must Divert More Foreign Investments to the Central

and Western Areas by Reforming Our Industrial Policy

It should be noted that foreign investments have genuinely played an important role in regional economic development. The speedy growth of China's coastal economy has been proportional to the concentration of foreign investments. But if these stopped flowing to the eastern areas, it is not inevitable that they would flow to the central and western areas. There exists a question of gradient development. When the coastal economy develops to a certain stage, and when the investment environment in the central and western areas have been improved, the advantages of exploiting the resources in these areas will increase their attraction to foreign capital. Therefore, we should think more how to guide foreign investments to inland by means of our industrial policy so as to lead China's regional economy toward balanced development.

Facing the growing acuteness of competitions in foreign investments internationally, the adjustment of China's macro-economic policy ought to increase its attractiveness and utilization of foreign investments. In the meantime, we must integrate the introduction of foreign investments with our gradual participation in the international market.

D. Efficiency Must Be a Priority in the Course of China's Development and Should Be Well Understood By Everyone

In an unbalanced regional economy with limited or scarce resources, we are apt to place those resources in projects and regions with the greatest potential for development, large scale production, and investment returns. The economic strength of these regions will then be strengthened and the economic development of the entire area will be promoted. In its process of reform, China first built a series of model economic centers in coastal areas which gives an impetus to the development of other regions.

In today's China we confront a situation where resources are not abundant, there is a very low average rate of distribution per person, the resource structure is not rational, and the quality of resources is not high. Therefore, China's economic development must be based on the efficient utilization of resources, including giving preference to develop superior regions which will in turn produce more. The problem of unbalanced regional development has been properly handled in the process of reform.

E. National Policy Must Guarantee Coordinated Regional Development

If a policy which pursued the aim of "balanced development of all regions" was called "balanced policy" (as was the one in force before reform and opening) then the regional policy China adopted in the 80s may be called "unbalanced policy." The policy consisted of two basic fundamentals. First, the Central Government gave more investment to places where more economic benefits could be achieved. This enabled the coastal regions with superior sites to get increased investments. The second feature of this policy was the state granting a series of preferential policies designed to speed up the economic development of the coastal regions, such as allowing them to retain foreign exchange, introducing foreign investment, more powers to import and export, tax relief, freedom to keep a larger portion of their profits, rights to make greater investment, and increased latitude to approve their own programs.

We define a policy of "adequate balance" as the policy which neither seeks an immediate abolition of all gaps in regional development nor lets such gaps go unnoticed and unchecked. This policy is one which will not "add fuel to the fire," but rather adopt measures to control such widening gaps, and continue to see the economic expansion of promising regions. Specifically such a policy would include:

1) In fact the policy of "adding flowers to the brocade" (or making what is good still better) has already started to weaken. At the beginning of reform and opening, it was necessary to make some adjustments in investment policy favourable to the coastal regions and grant them certain preferential policies in order to allow them to take the lead in the reform. The long term implementation of the policy of "balanced economy" had produced a

poor investment climate and this situation had to be changed. But today, that policy has basically accomplished its historical mission.

Here we should reiterate that this "adding flowers to the brocade" is to be maintained and not completely abolished. The state may still retain certain preferential policies for the Special Economic Zones which continue to develop at a higher rate and carry out important and special functions. In addition there exist backward regions even in coastal areas and it is resonable for them to receive some special consideration from the state. In the meantime, "weakening" should be looked upon as a process—a process in which the scope of this policy and its intensity is gradually diminishing.

2) For the sake of preventing further widening of regional difference, it is necessary to give more assistance and support to the backward regions by the state. We should think of making such assistance and support an institutional procedure. For example, it may be possible to prescribe in the state budget a certain percentage as a special fund for assisting and supporting backward regions. But it is clear that economic support is not the fundamental solution to the problem. More work has to be done in the opening and reform for these backward regions.

III. The Development of Regional Economy and Social Development

A. The Future Driving Force of Chinese Economic Society Should Be Urbanization Not Industrialization

In the 80s the driving force was industrialization. But the future depends on the coordination and cooperation of economic regions which will establish the superiority of urban centers.

Now the coastal development should be promoted by urbanization instead of industrialization. In urbanization the emphasis is the rearrangement of industries. The city ought to be a city, and not a center of manufacturing plants. It should emphatically develop the tertiary industry, while transplanting major industries to the nearby countryside.

B. The Coordination of Urban-Rural Relations Is Imperative to Regional Development

In the course of regional development there exists a degree of contention between urban and rural areas and between regions. In the current situation a coordination of these forces is imperative for the development of regional economy. The urban economy should be gradually adapted to the needs of the marketization of rural economy while state-owned enterprises become able to consume agricultural products whose prices have been freed up by the reform.

In the development of regional economy, we have to transform step by step the agricultural effects on industry and then the industrial effects on agriculture so as to achieve an exchange of goods and services at parity. On the question of urban-rural relations, macroeconomic policy should avoid the tendency of itself fostering urbanization. The development of regional economy will be pushed forward by coordinating the relations between the countryside and the cities.

C. Attaching Importance to Economic Development While Ignoring Social Development Must Be Ended

The unbalanced development of regional economy and society is a major problem in China at present. Although the reform and opening policy is beneficial to advance the overall development of the economy and creates a good foundation on which further advances can be built, it does not handle the relative sluggishness of social development. If this is not well handled it will sooner or later damage economic growth. Thus social development must achieve a plateau with economic development. There is a saying internationally that you can "overreach your growth." This means that you cannot simply talk about "economic" indicators alone, but must include social indicators such as the quality of the standard of living. Otherwise the scene become irrational. Therefore, the coordinated development of economy and society is of primary importance to regional economy.

IV. Regional Development and Special Economic Zones

A. The Position and Role of the Special Economic Zone in China's Economy

Importance should still be attached to the special role of the special economic zone in China's regional economy.

The South China economic belt where the five special economic zones are situated and which links Hong Kong, Macao, Taiwan and the Asia-Pacific region has become the most active economic sphere in the world today. There is no other area, on an immediate basis, which could replace the position and role of these special economic zones in the growth and development of China's regional economy.

A new pattern of opening has appeared throughout the world. The tendency toward the liberalization of trade and integration of regional economy is more obvious than ever. The "Bogor Declaration" of the Asia-Pacific Economic Cooperation stated the purpose "to achieve the goal of free and open trade and investment in the Asia-Pacific region no later than the year 2020." The founding of the European Common Market, the establishment of the free trade region among the US, Canada and Mexico, the gradual formation of the sphere of economic cooperation between China's mainland, Hong Kong and Taiwan, and the general development of economic integration are all parts of the overall world trend.

The special economic zone is an important instrument to carry out China's macroeconomic policy. Its function is still necessary under current conditions. Its original purpose to serve as a "window" and "experimental field" have largely been achieved. But it still have a large role to play as an instrument of macroeconomic policy in the country's future development.

Equal competition is a basic principle of the socialist market economy. But the key to the success of these SEZs was to allow them to have more flexibility in reform and opening and greater decision-making power in economic management. The burden upon these zones will become more arduous as we seek to speed up the transition of the entire country towards market economy. Therefore it is imperative to maintain the privileges that will allow these zones to fulfill these obligations.

At present the question has been posed as to whether it is necessary for the special economic zones to exist after China's restoration to the GATT. It should be clear that there is no contradiction between China's restoration of its position as a signatory state to the General Agreement on Tariffs and Trade and its participation in the World Trade Organization and the existence and development of the special economic zones. Why? In the first place, preferential policy and the more open system practised in the special economic zones are in complete accord with the GATT aims of lowering tariffs and reducing tariff barriers in order to bring about the world free trade. Secondly, no article in the GATT prohibits any country from opening up special economic zones (free trade zones), and the non-discriminatory and transparency principles are not leveled at special economic zones. Thirdly, there are more than 1,000 special economic zones in the world at present and many of which have been established by countries and regions belonging to the GATT.

China's SEZs will play an important role in the process of China's more extensive opening to the outside world. Because they have already achieved a degree of competitiveness in the international market, these zones can be a link in conducting the country as a whole toward participating in a unified world market and in international economic cycles. Using them in this way is the correct choice by China in adhering to the practice of market economy and quickening its advance toward the international market.

The role of the SEZ in stabilizing China's macroeconomy must be correctly evaluated.

China must maintain overall economic stability if it expects to achieve a smooth transition to a market economy. The emergence of the SEZs has certainly influenced the rest of the economy, but it is important to correctly analyze this influence. For example, it is said that it has been a major factor in increased prices nation-wide. In fact, it has not exerted such an influence. The reform of grain purchasing and marketing was initially led by the SEZs and coastal regions. But this did not cause any increase in grain prices—in fact, by greatly expanding the grain market, it was instrumental in aiding the nation-wide reform of grain prices which actually stabilized these prices and in some cases lowering them.

In Guangdong and other open coastal regions, we saw in recent years a reduction in areas cultivating "water grains." This did cause somewhat of an increase in grain prices, however limited it might have been. The fact is that these influences should neither be ignored nor exaggerated. And the answer, at any rate, is to allow these SEZs to make their own decisions and to grow at their most optimum rate according to the framework of the market economy.

On the contrary, regional blockades will cause increases in the price of grains. In the meantime, the coastal region and the special economic zones should be properly allowed to import grains to balance the market price. This helps stabilize markets across the country.

In the second place, an analysis must be made of the SEZs' effect on general inflation as a result of the inflow of foreign investment. In fact, it was exactly this foreign investment that created the speedy development of the SEZs. According to statistics, the value of industrial output of foreign enterprises has accounted for more than 50 percent of the total in SEZs. Compared to the recent recession of the world economy this sustained high speed growth of China's economy offers excellent opportunities for foreign investment. The enormous inflow of international capital has given rise to the relative increase of the supply of both domestic and foreign currencies, which has a certain influence on inflation. But it should be noted that the proportion of the input of foreign investment is very small in comparison to overall social investment in which the direct investment of the state accounted for 60-70 percent. Up to the end of 1994, the amount of foreign investment introduced by the Special Economic Zones was in fact only 18.4 percent of the total amount that was actually utilized. So its influence on inflation was just next to nothing.

The key to effective macro-control over foreign investment is to restrict its use in speculative areas. This alone will avoid large fluctuations in the economy; as to its direct input to the production area, not only should it not be restricted but should be encouraged and supported, particularly export-oriented direct investment by foreign businessmen.

In the third place, we must understand how to carry out effective macro-regulation within the special economic zones. The development of the market economy needs macro-regulation, and the special economic zone is no exception. The success of macro-regulation is generally measured with reference to the standard and rate of economic development. As it relates to SEZs, macro-regulations should promote their speedy growth with the goal of enabling them to play a more effective role in national macro-regulation. For example through demonstrating superior efficiency and increased growth they could make greater contributions to central finance funds. They could also directly foster improvements in interior regions and spur on inland economic development.

We must correctly evaluate the actual role China's SEZs should play in the transition from unbalanced development to balanced development.

China is now situated at the beginning of a transition from unbalanced regional development to balanced regional development. The current situation of large gaps in the progress of different regions is an existing reality and the conflicts and problems arising from this have received much attention. The actual role of the SEZs in this situation must thus be re-evaluated.

The actual function and purpose of SEZs was laid out by Deng Xiaoping when he pointed out that areas where conditions are more favorable will develop first while other areas will develop later. The former will spur on the latter, and finally they will arrive at common prosperity.

This is exactly what has occured. As the coastal areas have

developed, these SEZs have provided the initiative to spark the development of the interior. And this function will have even more importance in the near future.

Secondly, what actual effect has the special economic zone made in establishing the national unified market? In this transition, the key process is the breaking down of trade barristers, gradually establishing a unified market, and, in the course of the latter, strengthening the economic links and cooperation between the different regions. A national unified market would enable products and elements to move freely—resources can be disposed of optimumly to the advantage of many areas. In this process there is no basic conflict between SEZs and the interior—in fact, they completment each other. Economic development in the SEZs will require, after a certain time, an adjustment to their industrial structures. Their plants will need to be upgraded and the old generation of products will be replaced by new ones. The logical placement of such enterprises is where costs are lower and resources more plentiful. This will greatly benefit both the SEZs and the interior. Funds will be channelled into the interior from the SEZs; groups of industries will be transferred inland from the special economic zones; the SEZs will find it in their interests to set up training facilities; administrative talent will also move back—thus the interior and the special economic zones gradually will form closer cooperative relations.

New targets must be set to define the direction of the further development of China's Special Economic Zones.

Undoubtedly, any further development of SEZ must conform to international practices. The special economic zones of different countries in the world, also called free economic areas, are usually non-tariff areas under the supervision of local customs agencies. After China's "restoration" to the GATT, the process of opening of the country to the outside world will be reinforced. For the sake of maintaining and developing the function and role of the special economic zone, we should define it according to international terminology: i.e. an economic zone "beyond the reach of customs." When the SEZ will be elevated to a non-tariff area is another question.

At present, the five special economic zones are poised to turn from "within the reach of the customs" to "beyond the reach of the customs." They enjoy site superiority (proximity to Hong Kong, Macao, Taiwan and Southeastern Asia) good links to international markets, superior infrastructure and production efficiency. After years of effort (still continuing) living facilities are better and a sound industrial base has been created including modern electronics, textiles, light industry, machinery, chemical engineering, construction materials and food processing trade; as well as providing good conditions for the building of legal and administrative systems.

The further development of China's SEZs can be accomplished by using patterns which have proven successful in other countries. The world's special economic zones are divided up into specialized kinds such as free ports, free trade areas, export processing areas, scientific industrial areas, and others. The selection of such a pattern must be done on the basis of the existing conditions and advantages of the SEZs themselves.

To bring these zones to a higher stage of development it will be vital to reinforce past successful actions, improve the quality of administration and products, and explore and exploit untapped potentials.

For example, the Hainan special economic zone should fully take advantage of its resource superiority, further develop tropical agriculture, tourism and its processing industry in order to establish a comprehensive special economic zone. Shenzhen should, on the basis of its existing industrial system, endeavour to develop export-oriented industry. Establishing a customs-free SEZ will inevitably accomplish a strong link between the national economy and the world economy. As a stopgap measure, Shenzhen and Zhuhai special zones should closely connect with Hong Kong and Macao so as to evolve as close (and as early) an economic integration as possible. Xiamen should do the same with Taiwan; Hainan should strengthen its economic cooperation with the southeast Asian countries; and the Shantou special zone should give fuller play of the advantage of its relations with the great numbers of overseas Chinese.

B. The Hainan Special Zone Should Be Further Enhanced

Hainan's economy had swiftly developed since it became a province and set up as a special zone in 1988. Within the first three years, the investment of fixed assets was 17 billion yuan, greatly exceeding the total national investment in the area's state enterprises over the previous 30 years since the founding of the People's Republic of China. In 1993 alone, the investment of fixed assets reached 16.94 billion. Five years after the establishment of the Hainan province and special zone, it had accomplished the first target of reaching the domestic average level of development put forward then by the Central Government. The gross value of national production of the province in 1993 was 20.4 billion yuan, increasing 2.7 times over that in 1987 before the establishment of the province, with an average annual growth above 20 percent. It seems that it is entirely possible for Hainan, within 20 years, to fulfill its target of catching up with the development level Taiwan enjoyed in the 80s.

Hainan's distinctive natural resources must be exploited.

The real superiority of Hainan lies in its resources. The Hainan island is known as the "treasure island" for its very abundant in natural resources. It has a total area of 3.38 million hectares, occupying 42.5 percent of the tropical area of the country. It is also China's most productive tropical region, cultivating such economic crops as rubber, coconut, oil palm and others. It is also the leading producer of the four major medicines grown in the south. There are 600 thousand hectares of wasteland not yet being exploited. The overall output of cultivated land is rather low but has great potentialities. Hainan also has rich mineral resources of which more than 60 kinds have been proven. The malachite iron ore there is the richest iron ore in Asia, occupying 71 percent of the reserves of the country; zircon occupies 60 percent of the reserves. Deposits of petroleum and natural gas are also abundant. Two of the three oil fields in the South China Sea (Yingehai and Bac Bo Bay) are within Hainan's territorial waters. Adding the development of the Qiongbei oil field on the island itself, the yield of petroleum and natural gas will be quite considerable. Hainan is surrounded by sea, its coastline being 10.1 percent of that of the China mainland, so it has large varieties of sea products. It is richly endowed by nature in tropical resources, enjoying the fame of "Garden of Hundred Fruits," and is one of largest producing areas of tropical and sub-tropical fruits. It has great potentialities in agricultural resources and is ideal place to develop high-yielding, fine-quality and high-efficiency modern agriculture. It also has distinctive tourist attraction being a virgin land which still preserves its natural tropical scenes and bewitching landscapes and one that is situated at the same latitude as Hawaii.

Hainan's abundant natural resources are unique in the country. If they are fully exploited they will not only promote the development of the island itself, but will give a tremendous boost to the national economy as well.

Hainan's special geographical location has given it a strategic position both in opening up to the outside world and in national defence.

Hainan is situated at the hinterland of the Asian-Pacific region and its geographical location is very important. As a sea link, it is China's forward position possessing the shortest sea routes to Europe, Africa, Australia and the south Asian countries. It also has the potential to become the converging point for air, sea and land communications.

Hainan is also China's southern gate, and important outpost of coastal defence. After the founding of the People's Republic, an upsurge of development and construction was launched there but in the end the closed economic pattern that was adopted caused a backward state of economy which is inappropriate with the demands of national defence. The establishment of Special Economic Zone has greatly improved its economy and increased its strength of national defence.

In Hainan it is possible to establish a "greater special zone" by wider opening.

The fundamental way to make Hainan a "greater special zone" is to speed up the building of a highly open system of market economy.

Since the acceleration of the pace of the reform and opening throughout the country in 1992, the early policy advantages of Hainan as a special economic zone in comparison to its other sister provinces have been greatly eroded. This has been particularly so after the implementation of reforms in the system of central finance and taxation, the banking system, the system of planning and investment, and the system of foreign trade.

The Hainan special economic zone is confronting challenges from all directions of the country. The influence of the state has become increasingly evident in Hainan with the country's overall opening to the outside world together with its macro regulation over investment in fixed assets. Hainan has made some progress in the past seven years, but its economy as a whole is still very weak. In order to realize Deng Xiaoping's strategic concept and great intentions concerning Hainan when he said, "It will be really terrific if Hainan Island is to be earnestly developed," we must set up a market economy system conforming to the reality of Hainan, in accord with international practices, and able to attract large foreign investments.

The Hainan special economic zone is also confronting a new challenge from some neighboring countries which are competing with it to work out more free and more open economic policy, energetically set up free trade areas, and guarantee free economic regions or free ports. These have become China's strongest rivals with regard to the opening policy, attracting foreign capital and foreign technology by their preferential policies and special economic zones. Without a more open system established Hainan will continue to compete with these other countries at a distinct disadvantage.

Being isolated on the sea, Hainan's island economy gives it both superiority and limitations—both very conspicuous. Countries of this kind have developed in a thousand different patterns over the world, but the most successful of all are China's Hong Kong and Taiwan. We should learn the lessons from the success of their economic development and use the rights already conferred on Hainan by the Central Government, such as the right of legislation and the right of experiment, in order to incorporate already tried and proven laws into Hainan's patterns.

Hainan is in the most advantageous position to set up a maximum degree opening-oriented system of market economy.

Viewed from its geographical position, natural resources and the general policy superiority, Hainan has better conditions than other special zones or development regions to achieve a wide fast and active market system.

The conditions of reform in Hainan are relatively better than those of other special zones and regions. Before it became a province, its proportion of investment from the state was rather small, it had only a few small-scale state-run enterprises, and its contribution to the GDP was only 0.68 percent in 1993. Therefore there was little opposition to intensifying its economic reform.

To be "more open" is the guiding principle of Deng Xiaoping's strategy of building up the special zones. To make Hainan really a "bigger special economic zone" requires not ordinary opening, more open—this means differently from other regions. International thinking acknowledges the "free trade area" as the most successful pattern in an opening-oriented market economy. In building such a system in Hainan, we should learn from and boldly adopt the basic policy of other free trade areas, endeavor to accomplish the free passage of commodities, capital, and personnal both into and out of the zone, and gradually turn Hainan into one of the most open areas in the Asia-Pacific region.

Further breakthroughs shall be made in the opening policy through development of Hainan's natural resources.

The real superiority of Hainan lies in its resources. It would be "really terrific" if its unique resources could be fully exploited and utilized. Such programs could attract both foreign and domestic capital.

In the field of the development of tourism:

1) There are many things which could be done to attract additional capital for the development of tourist programs and the construction of tourist facilities.

Business magnates and big financial groups (foreign and domestic) can be invited to participate in the building of large projects, including airfields, ports and other infrastructure facilities. Foreign capital could be utilized to build some new, original and large-scale recreational centers like the Disneyland of the U.S. This would raise the quality of Hainan tourism and make it more appealing to the international tourism market.

Foreign capital must be increased and better utilized. New ways to attract and use it must be worked out, such as building hotels by joint investment and solely foreign investment. Only in this way, tourism of Hainan can take a great leap forward.

Flexible policies may be adopted in attracting domestic capital. For instance, Chinese merchants could have taxes on their enterprises waived until after starting to make profits from those enterprises.

2) Make Hainan a paradise for commodity-purchasing. The earnings of foreign exchange by sales of tourist articles in Hainan in 1993 was only 3.2 percent of the total earnings of the tourist industry that year. In comparison this percentage gets as high as 20 percent to 60 percent in more developed tourist areas. Of course there are great differences between Hainan and the famous international tourist spots, but this shows the great potentialities that Hainan could exploit in this respect.

Therefore, we must fight for more tariff protection for the island, thus establishing a superiority of low priced commodities. More tourist articles of high additional value and special features should be produced and an international duty-free commercial area opened up. By imitating the practice in France half of the duties levied on purchases may be returned to a tourist group upon its departure. Through the use of joint ventures and exclusively foreign funded enterprise, large-scale duty-free bazaars in Hainan and Sanya can be set up.

3) The exploitation of tourist resources depends on the support and cooperation of financial institutions. For example we must set up local joint-stock financial companies with the major purpose of supporting the tourism industry, and must establish a Hainan tourist development fund in order to promote tourism both within the country and abroad. Hainan tourist development bonds can also be issued.

4) The entry and exit procedures can be simplified and

tourist recreational activities enriched. Some countries practise extraordinarily simplified procedures of exit and entry, even extending "visa free" privileges to people from tourist-source countries. Hainan should enact similar measures and create flexible and convenient conditions for prospective tourists and develop healthy, appealing and exciting programs. The motto is to attract more and more tourists by every possible means, increase their recreational consumption while they are here, and prolong the duration of their stays.

5) Get governmental management functions to fully support this. For example, a Hainan Tourist Management Institute is preparing to be established and in cooperation with international organizations high quality tourist professionals will be trained. Hainan is perfectly suited to become a center of international conferences like Bandung. It needs only government support to make this happen.

In the field of developing modern agriculture, Hainan's agricultural resources possess tremendous potentialities, and its real superiority lies in agriculture.

The development of modern agriculture will lay a better foundation for the advance of tourism, the processing industry and trade. A "green highway" which integrates economic development with environmental protection can be constructed in the process of accelerating the agricultural development in Hainan. This will exert an important influence not only on China but on the rest of the world as well.

1) Hainan may further extend its opening, raise the amount of foreign capital it utilizes and set up more comprehensive agricultural development areas.

2) Hainan may work hard to introduce foreign experience, techniques and means of production in the development of modern agricultural systems.

3) Stress should be placed on developing export-oriented modern agriculture, giving emphasis to the horticulture industry with fruits and vegetables as its chief products. We can turn this treasure island into a big plate of fruits for the hinterland and big food baskets for the international market to satisfy demands both

at home and abroad.

4) Conglomerates should be developed which integrate trade, industry and agriculture and make production, processing and marketing a coordinated process. Through the increased efficiency possible in such operations Hainan can take the lead in earning foreign exchange through agriculture.

5) The existing farms may be reformed by introducing foreign capital. Right of export for these farms should be given so they can participate directly in international competition.

In the field of opening up the sea, the trip to Hainan's prosperity can be hastened if a few extra strides are taken from the land towards the sea. Strategically Hainan's opening can be greatly bolstered by modernizing the marine industry and turning the island into a marine province.

1) The rich offshore deposits of petroleum and natural gas must be exploited. Local authorities must be granted the rights to do so including the right to introduce and utilize foreign capital for joint exploration.

2) Coorperation with Taiwan should be promoted to foster commerce and co-action in respect of their mutual marine interests.

3) Marine communication and transportation should be developed so as to promote its development and opening.

The work stress should be put on the economic cooperation between Hainan and Taiwan. The potential scope for increased cooperation between Hainan and Taiwan is large.

1) Innovative proposals for general agricultural cooperation should be put forward and brought to fruition. Efforts should be made to gain more assistance from Taiwan for agricultural funding and new technologies. Cooperation should be strengthened in the agricultural processing industry as well as in marine fishing.

2) Emphasis must be placed on attracting Taiwan's big financial groups and enterprises to initiate a new round of investments.

3) The intermediary function of international organizations should be brought into full play in order to bypass any artificial obstacles still existing on the two islands.

4) The direct exchanges in mail, trade, air and shipping services between the two sides of the Taiwan Straits is inevitable and Hainan ought to go ahead and take the lead in initiating these exchanges between the two islands.

5) Hainan should take the lead in treating Taiwan merchants as members of the nation and allow Taiwan capital to freely flow into Hainan's financial and insurance businesses.

6) Taiwan's successful legislation may be borrowed for our use.

There should be new initiatives in the construction of the Yangpu development area because it affects Hainan's opening to the outside world.

1) Yangpu should be declared to be a "free port."

The State Council, in response to a proposal made in April 1992 to develop the Yangpu area in Hainan by absorbing foreign investment, has already said that a more open policy should be practiced in the Yangpu economic development area than in the free-trade zones and more flexible measures should be adopted with regard to the exit and entry of funds, commodities and personnel. Viewed from the standard patterns existing in the world market economy, the structure of "free port" is more open and flexible than the free-trade zone and meets this State Council recommendation.

However, for various reasons this direction was never implemented. Some thought Yangpu couldn't fulfil the objective because some policies were not enforced. So the first thing is to make efforts to solicit the Central Government to explicitly declare Yangpu a "free port" which will have the effect of getting the necessary policies implemented, restoring the confidence of foreign merchants, and re-establishing Yangpu's leading role in the country's process of opening up to the outside world.

2) Preferential policy should be adopted to encourage the input of domestic capital in order to absorb and stabilize foreign capital investment. Such policy would include allowing the entry and establishment of labor-intensive companies and supporting large enterprise by extending credit to them and reducing taxation.

3) Financial policy should be relaxed to allow foreign banks to set up branches in Yangpu and to permit foreign merchants to establish financial organs through investment. Both of these are capable of raising extensive funds to support the development and construction of Yangpu.

4) The government should, on its own accord, help the Yangpu Land Reclamation & Development Co. Ltd. settle its problems and extricate it from its predicaments. The government may also introduce foreign business magnates to Yangpu in order to support foreign merchants in successfully carrying out the development and management of large tracts of land.

The further opening of Hainan involves a number of problems, including that of the opening to internal investment—the key to this is the question of property rights. While extending internal and external investments, we must earnestly work to protect the interests of those enterprises which have already invested in Hainan but have run into difficulties as a result of the conditions mentioned above. There are also questions of law and social environment that must be tackled in the process of implementing the opening policy. Social security, for example, needs further strengthening.

C. The Development of World Economy Has an International Trend Towards Regionalization

Groups of countries linked by georaphic proximity or by other factors have integrated economically for their mutual benefit and protection. In line with this tendency we should push towards the formation of a Chinse System of Economic Cooperation between the Chinese mainland (especially the South China areas), Hong Kong, Macao and Taiwan. This idea has recently been receiving understanding and approval from more and more experts and scholars.

Since the CSEC would be a system, its members would interact, engage in mutual promotion, and establish some form of coordinating mechanism.

There would be different levels of collaboration: the first would include a systematic cooperation concerning bilateral or multilateral trade and investment agreements and would embrace any sort of cooperative trade or industrial plans by any inter-related enterprises or non-governmental bodies. Plans of cooperation could be formed on the basis of competition between enterprises in different regions or within the same enterprise.

The second level would involve the cooperation and coordination of industrial policy and structure set up by bilateral or multi-lateral parties specifically as it effects the market economy. This would include the industrial division and coordination of labour and, the adjustment of investment structure and the coordination of trade policy. Such policy cooperation and coordination can hardly be fulfilled by corporations alone, but would need to be assisted by government-supported civil bodies or semi-official organizations. The third level would involve the bilateral or multi-lateral exchange and cooperation concerning general long-term strategy and tactics. The accomplishment of this level would even more require the help of official or semi-official organizations, or at the very least guidance from government-supported civil bodies.

A model example of an fully open market economy exists in Hong Kong, and a similar mechanism has been gradually emerging in Taiwan over the past 40 or so years. The China mainland is now speeding up the transition from planned economy to market economy. The reform and opening of the economic system carried out on the China mainland in the past 16 years has achieved great successes. In the meantime, the Chinese Government's policy of "one country, two systems" has successfully solved the question of the return to China of Hong Kong and Macao; and the policy of "peaceful unification, one country and two systems" has laid a foundation for relations between the mainland and Taiwan. Therefore, the earlier small-scale and uncoordinated economic conditions between the mainland and Hong Kong, Macao, and Taiwan can be superceded by economic exchange and cooperation of great scope, relaxation of older policies and setting up civil coordinating mechanisms by all sides. Large numbers of manufacturing enterprises in Hong Kong and Taiwan have already expanded their operations to South China area on the mainland, gradually forming systematic industries in a trans-regional pattern of collaboration that can form the basis of the CSEC. As the China mainland is now accelerating its pace of reform it will undoubtedly vigorously push forward the formation and development of the Chinese System of Economic Cooperation. After the return of Hong Kong and Macao to the motherland in 1997 and 1999 a comparatively high level of this system will be in existence—for example, a unified common market will be established on this basis. The emphasis on the following period will be on economic cooperation between the mainland and Taiwan. As to what level this system will develop, that will be decided by the joint efforts of the Chinese people on both sides of the Straits.

The Chinese system of economic cooperation has a lot to do with the speedy establishment on the mainland of the institution of socialist market economy.

The most important tasks are as follows:

1) Competition and cooperation among the enterprises of the mainland and Hong Kong and Macao should be promoted.

The Chinese system of economic cooperation will progress by a series of stages and levels. From embryo it will grow to maturity. There may be some ups and downs in the overall process but the general trend will not change, simply because there is no force that can stand against the tendency of strengthening competition and cooperation among the enterprises concerned. As a practical way of buidling a foundation for the CSEC. private enterprises and civil bodies begin to plan and establish a stronger dialogue of cooperation. Of course, such cooperation could only be of preliminary and low-level, but one that could continually advance towards higher levels.

There is already a solid foundation for the further cooperation between the mainland and Hong Kong, Macao and Taiwan.

a) A much better relation of economic cooperation has already been established. From 1979 to the latter half of 1993, the China mainland had approved 134,000 foreign enterprises. The total investment by foreign merchants was 43.75 billion US dollars, among which the investment from Hong Kong and Macao occupied more than 70 percent and that from the Taiwan enterprises 7 percent. About 80 percent of the manufacturing industries of Hong Kong moved to the mainland, particularly to the coastal region in South China, thus forming a new economic and trade pattern of "a shop in the front and the factory in the backyard." The number of Taiwan enterprises which made investments on the mainland has exceeded ten thousand. Likewisely, many mainland enterprises (now over 1000) have invested in Hong Kong in recent years. By the end of 1991, the amount of investment made by mainland enterprises in Hong Kong came to about 16 billion US dollars. Particularly since China has accelerated its pace in reform and opening and defined the targets of the market economy, there has been an obvious increase in the cooperation between the mainland and Hong Kong, Macao and Taiwan, and the characteristics of the latter's investment in the former are large in scale, wide in range, long term and fast to develop. There may be a new leap in the cooperation of enterprises between the mainland and Hong Kong, Macao and Taiwan if things continue to develop in this direction. b) There are advantages possessed by the mainland and by Hong Kong, Macao and Taiwan that complement each other and are ripe for cooperative ventures in the interests of all sides. For example the enterprises of Hong Kong, Macao and Taiwan possess advanced science, technology and management experience. As a center of international financial services, Hong Kong has developed highly advanced marketing and financial systems and Taiwan owns considerable quantities of foreign exchange. All these are urgently needed for the development of mainland enterprises. But the mainland has supremacy in energy, minerals, both raw and processed materials, cheap labour and rich territorial resources which are needed by the enterprises of Hong Kong, Macao and Taiwan. The combination of each other's advantages could form the basis of a highly complementary economic relationship. Second, Hong Kong, Macao and Taiwan are facing the problem of transforming their industrial structure, and they need to greatly develop the scientific and technology-intensive industries. And in the process of upgrading their own industries it is also their desire to transfer their labour-intensive industries to the mainland. c) The enterprises of Hong Kong, Macao, and Taiwan are confronting the challenge and pressure of acute international competition. Regionalism and trade protectionalism in the world economy have caused shrinking markets and compels them to seek cooperation with the mainland in order to cope with the world economic situation. d) The historical, cultural, linguistic and geographical factors, together with the improvement of the environment on the mainland (particularly the coastal regions in South China) provide good conditons for further cooperation.

Other measures can also be taken to encourage the formation of the CSEC. The scale and scope of joint ventures between the mainland and Hong Kong, Macao and Taiwan can be broadened. Cooperation between inter-related enterprises in the same business or trade can be encouraged. Service organizations between the enterprises of the mainland and those of Hong Kong, Macao and Taiwan should be positively set up, like the enterprise association, society of promoting cooperation among enterprises, friendship association, etc. The role of civil bodies and semi-official organizations should be brought into full play in strengthening the cooperation among enterprises with regard to the contact, coordination, guidance and assistance.

2) We must promote the establishment of a unified market under the Chinese system of economic cooperation and extend its scope of economic cooperation.

Following the practice of the reform and opening policy on the mainland in the 70s, trade and economic exchanges between the mainland and the Hong Kong, Macao and Taiwan regions have been continually consolidated. Economic reports have shown that the proportion of export from Hong Kong and the mainland has risen from 3.3 percent of the world's total in 1986 to 4.9 percent in 1991. In the same five years 35.8 percent of the total growth in Asian exports came from the mainland and Hong Kong. Meanwhile, of the total international growth in exports 7.1 percent came from the mainland and Hong Kong. In Hong Kong trade with the mainland accounted for 84.8 percent in 1991. The mainland has become Hong Kong's biggest trading partner. Taiwan has also surpassed the US and become the second largest in its investment in the mainland. According to estimates the economic and trade growth between the two sides of the Straits will be 10 percent this year. Therefore, we can say that the economic development of the mainland and Hong Kong, Macao and Taiwan is inextricably bound together.

Following the return of Hong Kong and Macao to the motherland and the continued development of the proceeding of the unification of China, the establishment of a unified market of the Chinese System of Economic Cooperation will promote the common prosperity and overall progress of the Chinese nation.

a) The circulation of capital must be given attention. Within a unified market, the circulation of capital must be free and unimpeded. Before such a system can be implemented it is necessary to settle several questions. The first is the free conversion of currencies. The Renminbi is not yet freely convertible, but it can be exchanged for Hong Kong dollars in Hong Kong, and Hong Kong dollars are likewisely acceptable in the coastal regions of South China and can be converted to Renminbi through the foreign exchange regulation center. Secondly a certan amount of coordination is required with regard to industrial policy to optimumly handle any conflicts of competition between regions. The third point requires the mutual establishment of financial organs between the mainland and the Hong Kong, Macao and Taiwan regions. Banks of foreign, Chinese and overseas Chinese capital are at present setting up their branches in China one after another; at the same time, China's banking system and financial organs are also opening their offices in Hong Kong. The establishment of joint-venture banks by Taiwan financial institutions on the mainland is encouraged and preferential policies will be provided. The mutual establishment of banks and financial organs will be in the interest of promoting the circulation of capital within the unified market.

b) The free circulation of commodities, otherwise known as free trade, is another basic requirement of unified market. Although the present amount of trade between the mainland and Hong Kong is quite considerable, most of the trade between the mainland and Taiwan goes through Hong Kong. The Chinese system of economic cooperation is required to adopt measures to carry out free trade and coordinate trading policies in the spirit of GATT. Direct trade between the mainland and Taiwan should be achieved. Trade between the two sides of the Straits ought to be direct and mutually complementary. Having to route all goods between Taiwan and the mainland through Hong Kong raises the cost of commodities, and wastes time in transit. It also adversely affects the quality of some commodities. A change in this situation is sorely needed.

c) The free circulation of labour between enterprises and regions has gradually become a reality that has come with the intensification of reform. The return of Hong Kong and Macao to the motherland calls for further development in this area. Taiwan's experience in economic development sets a good example for the mainland, especially for Hainan and the other provinces in the South China area. The mainland is not only in need of funds and qualified personnel from Hong Kong and Macao, but also their experience in successful management, techniques and advanced technology. The establishment of a unified market will create favourable conditions for the circulation of personnel. The questions which need immediate attention are: 1) How do we settle the free circulation of common personnel between the mainland and Hong Kong and Macao. Although this will become less of a problem as the day of their return to the motherland approaches it will still apply between the mainland and Taiwan. The second question involves the circulation of technical personnel and talented managers. The circulation of specialized experts should be allowed between the mainland and Hong Kong, Macao and Taiwan, so as to realize the optimized disposition of talented persons and resources in the unified market. A unified or interconnected labor market for labor services and talented persons should be established in order to create the necessary conditions for circulation of the labor forces and talented personnel.

3) The Chinese system of economic cooperation needs a set of laws and a legal basis for its formation and development. This system can hardly be formed and smoothly developed without

laws and regulations to serve as a basis. These laws must confirm the market system as the basic economic environment for enterprise and provide legal procedures for settling any disputes that may arise. The formation of the CSEC will certainly face a series of legal obstacles and problems due to the inherent differences in the legal systems and economies in the different areas. The laws of Taiwan, Hong Kong and Macao are based on the private ownership of capitalism, while the laws of the mainland are based on the public ownership of socialism. But while such differences will obstruct economic cooperation to a degree, this negative aspect will be greatly reduced by the mutual benefit both sides will derive from collaboration. Nevertheless, a sound legal system and firm basis of laws are paramount to the formation and development of the CSEC.

Chapter V
The Reform of the Social Security System in the Transition of China's Economy

With the development of China's socialist market economy, the need to reform the social security system has been gradually assuming greater importance. It has become a significant link in China's smooth transition to a market economy as well as a major factor influencing the success or failure of other reforms. The establishment of a new social security system must be in the interest of enhancing overall economic development, and the principle of "efficiency first with consideration to equity" must be the basis of any reform.

I. The Basic Thinking in Establishing the Modern Social Security System

A. The Importance and Necessity of the Reform of Social Security System

The 14th Congress of the Chinese Communist Party clearly pointed out that the establishment of socialist market economy is the basic goal in the reform of our economic system. This major breakthrough provides a basis for the establishment and perfection of China's modern social security system. Under the operation of market economy, the defects of China's traditional social security system have become increasingly conspicuous, which shows the need for reform in this field.

1) The reform of the social security system has created social conditions which allow enterprises of different types to more favorably compete in the market. Under the traditional social

security system, the state-run enterprise had to take care of the birth, old age, sickness and death of all its staff and workers, causing it to bear a heavy load and making it difficult to advance. On the contrary, private enterprises and enterprises started up with foreign capital can operate without any burden and develop swiftly. The problem is that there is no reliable security for the long term interest of their staff and workers, and this is disadvantageous to the stability and long range development of the enterprise.

2) The reform of the social security system will promote the intelligent utilization of the labour force and meet the needs of the adjustment of industrial structure. Under the operation of market economy, a rational utilization of labour is a key element in the optimum disposition of resources. Therefore, in the interests of maintaining competetive impetus and vitality in economic life we must establish a social security system that is advantageous to optimum utilization of manpower.

3) The reform of the social security system will rationally adjust the interests of the state, enterprise and individuals.

4) Social security must correspond to the level of economic development.

5) The imbalance of China's economic development requires social security of different types and levels instead of a unitary pattern.

6) Economic development requires a stable social environment, and the reform of the social security system means the creation of a social mechanism of stability. In the meantime it will additionally cultivate the social mechanism of incentive.

B. Reform of the Old-Age Pension System

1) The chief malpractice of China's present old-age pension system lies in a repayment of premiums that does not take into account rights and duties. In the past few years, the overall social planning of the old-age pension system had played a positive role in balancing the old-age pension burden of enterprises and promoting social stability, but such egalitarian overall planning failed to fully link up and coordinate each of the three principal

parts of the pension system, namely the insurer, enterprise and management organ. The operation of the overall planning of the system lacks inherent motivation and can only be maintained by administrative measures. This is the major problem which needs to be settled in the reform of this system.

2) China's old-age pension system is facing three options from which it must choose: The first one is to reform and perfect the existing pension system of overall social planning by means of enlarging its scope, raising its level, increasing social programs, adjusting the rate of overall planning expenses, and improving its measures in order to proceed to the transition to the provincial and national overall planning. The second choice is to transform gradually to the old-age pension system which has the individual account as its basis resulting from compulsory saving. The third is to start from the reality of the country and create a new pattern of pension system with Chinese characteristics in line with the development of market economy by utilizing the advantages and making up any deficiencies from the overall planning type and the individual account type.

The ageing problem of the population is proportionate to the level of economic and technological development. People live longer. But the effect of the existing old-age pension system is frequently to take from the poor in order to subsidize the rich. Funds extracted from regions where the populations is relatively younger but with a lower level of economic development are used to subsidize the regions where the population is more economically developed and facing a greater problem with the aged. In the deepening of the reform, this conflict is certain to become more pronounced and glaring if merely attempt to blindly upgrade the old-age pension system by transforming the burden to the provincial or national level without introducing an insurance system and adopting the mechanism of pensions.

3) Through the reform, we should transform the existing single-level pension system of overall social planning into a multi-level one of basic insurance plus supplementary insurance. This will meet people's different needs of security of the pension system.

State enterprises will no longer shoulder the entire burden —it will be shared by the state, enterprise (employer) and the individual. The basic premium will be chiefly paid by the enterprise with payments by individual workers as auxiliary. The starting point of individual payments should be low. It should be introduced step by step at the time of salary adjustment, increase of income and improvement to bear increased financial responsibility. The supplementary insurance is divided into two kinds: the enterprise supplementary insurance and the individual supplementary insurance, both dovetailing into a system of accumulation funds in individual accounts. The enterprise supplementary insurance can be decided at present by the enterprise itself in accordance with its economic benefits. When enterprise benefits reach a certain level its supplementary insurance system will be governed through legislation. The individual supplementary insurance will link up with the basic insurance by compulsory saving and the standard payments of which will be gradually developed from low to high.

The way in which the insurance system is managed must be changed. In the first place the old-age pension fund of mutual assistance must be integrated with the individual old-age pension fund. We should legally define the individual's property right, keep separate accounts and independent calculation, and raise the clarity of accounting in order to strengthen the confidence of the insured. We should enter the basic premium into the account of the fund of social mutual assistance, the ownership of which belongs to all the insurers, and enter the supplementary premium into the account of individual old-age pension fund, the ownership of which belongs to the individual. The use of these funds must strictly abide by the old-age pension legislation and the regulation of the management. We ought to open for every insurer an old-age pension account and prescribe a life-long fixed coding in common use throughout the country. We should endeavour to fulfil the socialization of the management of old-age insurance and the modernization of management measures.

Concerning the pattern of the repayment of the insurance, the current fixed-sum repayment of pension will be changed to a structural repayment of basic insurance amount plus supplementary insurance amounts; at retirement the payment will be changed to one which links the repayment of basic insurance amount with the payment of premium. The repayment of basic insurance amount will be exactly based on the index according to the average payment of the worker's salary during his period of employment, and the proportion of repayment depends on the length of the period of insurance and payment of premium. The individual old-age insurance amount accumulated in the individual account will be, when the insurer retires, transformed to the supplementary old-age pension calculated according to the average man's life span, and it may be drawn monthly for the whole life. If the insurer goes abroad or dies before retirement, the whole accumulation of his individual account will be handed back in a single payment to himself or the directly-related members of his family.

For promoting the smooth transition from the old to the new pension system, different ways to treat the insurer can be applied. For example, applying a new system for new people, old measures for old people, and interim measures for intermediary people. The so-called "old people" means those people who have already retired at the time of the reform, and they will continue to enjoy the retirement treatment as prescribed in the document Guo-Fa (1978) No. 104; the so-called "new people" are those contract workers and provisional workers who participate at present in the overall planning pension system, as well as those who work after the practice of the reform, and the old-age pension regulation as prescribed by the new program will apply to them all; the so-called "intermediary people" are those workers who are in their tenure of office at the time of the practice of the reform, and they can choose either the old or the new measure as they like.

4) The reform of the old-age pension system is a social project which will change the relationship of distribution in ways that will impact on several generations of people. As a kind of transferring payment, the old-age pension aims to realize, so far as the working people are concerned, a balance of consumption in life through the form of insurance; as for the society, its aim lies in

ensuring the workability of a system when seeks to balance income and expenditure in different periods—funds raised today through the insurance system will be expended at a later time in order to provide for basic life needs of the aged people. Therefore, before the implementation of the reform, a qualitative and quantitative analysis must be made including metioulous calculations of the long-term effects of this program. As much as possible the payments and accumulations of the old-age pension premiums should be made to correspond to the economic developmental level of that region, population development and the financial-bearing ability of the state, enterprise, and workers. A certain margin should be left for the old-age pension fund to guard against any unforseen crisis concerning the problems of the aged.

C. On the Reform of the Medical System

1) There exists both waste and malpractice in the current medical system.

a) It lacks any control mechanism on medical expenses, so there is a serious waste of medical resources. China's present medical system consists of: "The patient consults the doctor; the doctor dispenses the prescription; and the state (enterprise) pays the money." In this system, all three factors are disconnected. This system results in the enormous increase and waste of medical expenses.

b) It lacks the mechanism to bear the cost of severe illness. This places increasingly heavy burden on the state and the enterprise. With medical expenses being solely born by enterprise, those enterprises which have relatively less personnel and low economic benefits can only afford to deal with medical treatments for general diseases. Once a patient contracts a critical illness, the enterprise is frequently unable to bear the medical expenses.

c) It lacks effective management and supervision over medical services. Some hospitals have adopted a practice of "business management" in recent years which they pursue solely for economic profit. Some doctors dispense prescriptions as "a favor," and others have taken this opportunity to promote the sales of medicines which have no curative effect but are capable of making big profits and from which they can personally benefit. This has caused a rapid rise in medical expenses which exceeds both the state's financial growth and corporate profits.

2) The outlet of the reform of the medical system.

a) We have to set a long term target for China's medical insurance system. The basic principles for the reform of medical insurance system are as follows: a. Enterprises of different kinds of economic status and trade, and staff and workers of different status are all equal in their relationships to the medical insurance system. b. Medical expenses are to be fairly shared by the state, enterprise and individual. c. Basic medical treatment for staff and workers must be guaranteed but in the meantime, endeavours have to be made to overcome the waste of medical resources, and gradually carry out the restructuring of medical service and medical insurance. d. The reform of the medical insurance system, the internal reform of the medical service centers and the institutional reform of the medicinal market should be interrelated.

b) The expenses of medical insurance are to be paid jointly by the enterprise (employer) and staff and workers, but mainly by the former, while individual payments should depend on the individual ability of the worker to pay. Owing to the different conditions in different regions, it is not appropriate to fix a unified ratio of payment.

c) In the outlay of medical insurance expenses, priority should be given to serious sickness. In this way, it guarantees the basic treatment of critically ill patients. Medical treatment is different from old-age insurance. When a worker has a disastrous or incurable disease, one can't afford to pay the medical expenses by himself or herself. So in this case we must rely on the society to secure normal medical treatment. Only by doing this, will the basic medical treatment of the staff and workers may be genuinely guaranteed.

d) Management of social medical insurance has to be strengthened. Improved management of the social medical insurance system is one of the keys for the successful introduction and implementation of this reform. Special medical insurance departments should be established to perform a unified management. There must be an effective control of the medical supply from the pharmaceutical departments and medical treatment centers, as well as the establishment of a mechanism of reliable supervision, examination and restraint. We should adopt administrative, economic and legal measures to govern and straighten up the medical and pharmaceutical trade and medical treatment centers.

e) Like other social insurances, the medical insurance system needs legislation to standardize and regulate its operation. We must strictly distinguish the rights and duties of the social management organ, medical service center, enterprise, and the staff and workers, and define their respective scopes of functions, so as to enable the medical insurance system to be legally effective, and then everybody will have laws and regulations to go by.

f) The reform of the public medical system should be carried out simultaneously with the reform of the medical insurance system. There should not be too much difference between the medical treatment of the two in order to prevent the transference of medical consumption toward the side which provides a higher level of security.

g) We must control a sky-rocketting growth of medical expenses, stop the waste of medical resources, strengthen the workers' consciousness of individual payment of expenses and at the same time regulate and bring under restraint the hospitals and medical and pharmaceutical trades.

h) We should adhere to the policy of making "prevention" the priority. Positive development is necessary in the work of prevention and health protection. Various kinds of mass sports activities should be supported so as to improve people's physique. In this way all people will benefit from an upgrade in quality of life and there will be a concomitant reduction in medical expenses. Therefore, it is necessary for us to build into the medical insurance system a mechanism to combine prevention with treatment.

B. Reform Is Also Necessary in the Insurance Systems of Unemployment and Industrial Injury

1) An unemployment and industrial injury insurance system should be gradually established, which is in conformity with the development of socialist market economy and stands in favor of equal competition of enterprises, rational circulation of the labor force and social stability. The unemployment insurance should correspond to the requirements of China's economic development and encourage unemployed persons to be re-employed in the shortest possible time. The earlier standard prescribed by the state, the traditional right of payment and security measures from the enterprise (employer) and the system of unemployment insurance which has been practiced among the staff and workers of state-run enterprises under the planned economy system should be thoroughly reformed.

2) According to the present actual situation, the reform of the insurance system of unemployment and industrial injury should be guided by the following principles:

a) The working people's basic right to life should be ensured.

b) Right and duty should be integrated. The insurance benefit should basically be tied to the cost of premium and we should dispense with the earlier egalitarian system.

c) Both equity and efficiency should be emphasized. The insurance of unemployment and on the job injury should not only secure the basic life of the unemployed and workers, but also favor the competition and circulation of the labor force. It should also reward production efficiency and safety in production. In particular, unemployment insurance should become a means to enhance the re-employment of the jobless as early as possible, to motivate and assure employment training, to provide job recommendations, and to promote the growth and perfection of the labor market so as to serve overall economic development.

3) We should enlarge the coverage of the insurance of unemployment and industrial injury including the participation of the staff and workers of different enterprises and institutions which practice business management. We should also extend the scope

171

of the coverage of unemployment relief, raise the socialization of the insurance, and lower the potential of industial risks.

4) In the raising of the funds for the insurance of unemployment and industrial injury payments should be set at a reasonable rate. The premium of unemployment insurance will be temporarily paid by the enterprise (employer) at present. A system of unemployment insurance by individual savings may be instituted in future to form the structural insurance of unemployment —this system has the benefit of reducing market risks. Insurance premiums for industrial injuries should be paid entirely by the enterprise according to a graduated scale based on the frequency of industrial accidents.

5) The term of repayment of the unemployment insurance amount will be shortened to 12 months from the existing 24 months, which will not only lower its cost but also encourage the enthusiasm of the unemployed for re-employment. The exact time for receiving unemployment premiums should be prescribed as one year—with an additional one month to cover the waiting period from the day of registration of unemployment. The time limit of payment should correspond with the number of years of insurance, and the standard of payment must take as the base the average monthly salary of the worker in the year previous to his unemployment. In order to conform to the actual situation of the development of market economy, the compensation of industrial injury should be made in one single payment except those who have permanently and completely lost their working ability in which cases they would get a disability subsidy payment every month.

II. Some Questions Concerning the Specific Operation of the Social Security System

China is just in the process of transition from planned economy to market economy. The establishment of China's social security system ought to meet and serve the needs of an economy in transition. Only by starting from this premise can we establish and perfect China's social security system, make it reliable, and have it fully play its role in promoting and ensuring the development of both the economy and the society.

According to the principle of the unity of right and duty, the repayment of the social insurance amount should be linked to the premium payments. At his retirement, a person would receive insurance payments based on what level of salary on which the insurer paid premiums during the course of his employment. This will ensure that the living standard of the insurer will not come down sharply at the time when he becomes incapable of working.

During the course of one's employment there will obviously be vast changes in both his salary level and the price of commodities. For the purpose of correctly calculating the salary level of the insurer and the contribution of payments he has made in the course of his employment, we should do our best to reasonably eliminate the influence of inflation on his old-age pension. In this we can draw on the experience of other countries which take an "indexed average salary" as the base of the insurance repayment amount. This is better to connect the old age insurance payments he receives with the actual value of the entire contribution he has made during his working life. It is the deferred repayment of the accumulated reward of his life's work, as well as the continuation and complement of distribution according to work.

There are a lot of advantages in doing this: a. It is a long-term encouragement to the insurer and promotes the increase of labor productivity in enterprises. b. It will improve the consciousness of social security among staff and workers, thus creating an internal incentive to better control the enterprise and to make social security payments on time. c. This kind of insurance payment will raise the clarity of the operating procedure of the old-age pension system. This will, in turn, place higher demands on the management work and service quality of the insurance system, and provide easier social supervision and participation in the management by the insurer. d. The calculation of payments based on an indexed salary will avoid the devaluative effect on old-age insurance amounts brought about by inflation, protect the interests of the insurer, improve the latter's confidence in the new system and thus enhance the smooth implementation of the reform of social security system. e. And it enables the insurer to be the main recipient of social security.

In order to ensure that the amounts of old-age insurance payments adhere to the principle of efficiency and equity, the method of calculating the indexed average salary on the basis of premium payments must be improved. For example, different rates may be paid according to the amount of income—like low rate of repayment for high income and high rate for low income. This will relatively reduce inordinately wide gaps in old age insurance due to the disparity in incomes.

There is also the question of the level of social security. In the reform of the social security system, both companies and individual workers and staff think that social security premiums are too high. So they demand a lower rate through reform. But at the same time the social security agencies lobby for an increase in rates, because they think that the rates are too low to meet the growing demands for social security services. Whether the premium rate of a region's social insurance is actually too high or too low depends not only on whether the local companies and staff can actually afford it, but also on whether the funds that have been raised are being used efficiently. For instance, how much is actually being spent on insurance repayments and how much on management expenses? What is the final accumulation of funds and is the share of each of the three sectors reasonable? A useful thing to do is to compare the premium rates and proportion of local retirees with the statistics of other cities. For example, in Shanghai the number of retirees comprise 31 percent of those insurers; for the premium rate of old-age insurance, the enterprise pays 25.5 percent of the total amount of salary and the individual pays 3 percent of his own salary, altogether 28.5 percent. In comparison with Shanghai, the proportion of retirees of some provinces is less than 15 percent of the workforce. In this case, its burden of old-age pension per head would be less than half that of Shanghai. If the rate is to be equal or exceeding that of Shanghai, we should consider that it is high.

Social security is a kind of transferring payment. The level of social security in a region depends on the local level of economic development and is restricted by the existing circumstances of population development. We must adopt a combined qualitative and quantitative measure to determine what is an appropriate security level for a particular region and this must be based on the economy, population and existing level of social security. In other words, we must proceed from the existing situation. At the beginning of the reform, it is generally not advisable to increase the burden being shouldered by national finance and enterprise, and individual payments likewise should start from low to high according to the individual's actual ability to pay.

In China's present system of social security, the level of medical security is far above the level of economic development. The public medical care and labor protection medical system originally set up in China are in fact a kind of free medical system entirely shouldered by the state and government enterprises. This exceeds the level of economic development of a country in its early stages of development. This medical security system has allowed too much expense in the treatment of minor sickness while frequently found lacking in more serious cases. There is a limit to what China's existing economic level can afford. We should use the medical insurance fund to guarantee the security of major sicknesses about which the insurer worries most.

The key to the full realization of social security reform is the establishment of a scientific and effective system of management. To this end, some problems which need to be settled are as follows:

1) How do we socialize management? We need to break down the barriers between different statuses of ownership, different ranks and relationships, different trades and industries, and different statuses of staff and workers (cadres and workers). We must create a unified social security system of management which covers the whole society at a unified rate on a unified base, and with unified regulations and control. All enterprises and the entire workforce are equal in the eyes of the social security system. This is necessary to ensure equal competition amongst

enterprises and optimum utilization of personnel.

2) How do we best separate the functions of the government's indirect macro-control and the direct control of business management organs.

The multi-level aspect of both the society and the social security system requires the management agency responsible for social security to be similarly structured. Social security agencies are divided into three levels:

a) The macro level of management. National and provincial social security committee must be established as the governmental institution responsible for regulating and enforcing the social security system. It would be charged with drafting laws, superintending, planning, and coordinating the social security system and also designing and proposing any needed social security reform programs. It would have a General Office, small but efficient, under it serving as the permanent organ responsible for the daily work.

There would also be oversight functions undertaken by relevant concerned departments, such as the departments of labor, public health, civil administration, personnel, finance, auditing, supervision. They would carry out administrative supervisory functions according to the respective scope of their individual zones of responsibility.

b) The intermediary level of execution. The provincial or municipal bureau of social security should be set up as the management organ of social security operations. They are in charge, under the leadership of the government (through the social security committee), of the specific operation of various social insurances, including the collection of the premium, management and repayment of the insurance, and providing the insured institutions and persons with security of high quality and efficiency.

c) The micro level of operation. The county bureaus of social security and basic-level offices of social assurance should be set up to take charge of the affairs of social security at the grassroots level, concretely engaging in the collection of premiums, repayment of insurance amounts and regional service. The basic-level offices of social insurance may also engage concurrently in social insurance, banking and saving business within the area of its jurisdiction, so as to promote banking through insurance and foster insurance by banking.

3) The administrative management of social security should be strictly separated from the management of the social insurance fund in order to ensure a stable increase of the fund at the same time as guaranteeing efficient supervision of the system.

We shall try combining insurance with banking in order to do a good job of managing the social insurance fund. We should invest in those programs which provide relatively good returns with less risk are beneficial to local economic development. Some ideas worth of consideration are: establishing a bank of social security espcially responsible for the investment management of the social security fund, use the social security fund to participate in the establishment of (through purchase of stock) a local "social development bank," or entrusting several non-banking institutions (through tender bidding) to act as our agent in the management of the social insurance fund.

The management of the social insurance fund is a key element in the management of social security. The success or failure of the social security system lies in whether the management of the social insurance fund is good or bad, whether its investment returns are high or low, and whether it can permanently maintain and even increase its value. According to the statistics of the Ministry of Finance, the labour departments throughout the country collected over 24.4 billion yuan in old-age insurance payments for the staff and workers of state-run enterprises in 1991, expended 20.2 billion yuan (in which 18.85 billion yuan were direct payments to retired veteran cadres), and was left with a balance for the year of 9.209 billion yuan which added to the previous balance came to 14.627 billion yuan. More than 3 billion yuan of the balance was used to buy state bonds and the rest was deposited in the bank. The collections of old-age insurance from the staff and workers of collective ownership enterprises was 5.084 billion yuan, expending 4.538 billion yuan (direct expenditure 4.332 billion yuan), and the unused balance that year was

0.546 billion yuan bringing the total accumulation up to 1.808 billion yuan. Revenues from the unemployment insurance fund was 0.837 billion yuan, expending 0.25 billion yuan (in which 24 million yuan expended directly for the relief of unemployed staff and workers), and the balance of the year was 0.587 billion yuan, increasing the accumulation to 2.518 billion yuan. Under the present economic situations, the actions of simply buying government bonds and depositing the remainder in the bank fails to realize the aim of ensuring the funds hold their value and even increase.

Both foreign and domestic experiences show that in order to maintain the value and achieve a marked gain in the fund, we must adopt the measure of integrating insurance with banking according to the guidelines given above.

4) Establish and strengthen the supervision of social security. One of the important marks of the maturity or immaturity of the local social security system is to see whether or not the supervision of social security in its region is sound and effective.

First of all, we should establish and strengthen all of the supervisory organizations connected with social security. This would include any councils set up by social security management organs, committees over social security funds, such as the old-age, medical service, unemployment and industrial injury funds. These would be composed of the representatives from the four sections: the governmental authorities concerned, staff and workers, the enterprise and relevant experts. A standardized operating and supervisory procedure should be established in order to ensure the efficient and conscientious management of the social security system.

Secondly, we should raise the visibility of all actions taken by management. Such actions must be democratized and brought into the open. The duty and working procedure of the various organs of social security should be clearly standardized and put under the examination and supervision of the insurer. The income, payment and balance of the social security fund, which the insurers are most concerned about should be made known to the public regularly so as to facilitate social supervision. Every insurer has the right to get information from the management organ about his premium payments, accumulation, current level of insurance repayment, and others, and ought to have a clear, timely and definite reply to any queries.

5) It is urgently necessary at present to standardize the relationships of social security and give strength and stability to those relationships through the power of law. Some of the points which must be clarified are: a. The relationship of right and duty between the various main participating bodies in ensuring security, namely the state, management organ of social security, enterprise (institution) and individual (staff and workers). b. The definition and adjustment of the relationships of the programs and levels of social security, ratio of premium payment of various social insurances and the standard of repayment of the social insurance amount. c. The definition and adjustment of the relationships of the establishment, function, duty, disbursement of expenses and the working procedure. d. The relationship of the collection and payment of the social security fund, i.e. the raising, management, payment and investment operation (including its program, principle, distribution of profits, and responsibility of risks) of the various social security funds, the proportion of allowable management expenses for supervising various social insurances, their scope of use and the means of payment. e. The relationship of supervision of social security, as well as of punishment in case of any violation of the law of social security.

Basic social security legislation is to be standardized and broadly issued by the state. Provincial authorities can work out rules for the implementation of various social security systems according to the basic legislation and their own actual conditions. Our target is that there will be laws and regulations to cover every contingency, and that we will be able to reduce if not eradicate all man-made alterations and opinionated decisions in the enforcement of administrative regulations. In this way we hope to overcome such things as "gracious grants" or "bestowals" in security repayment, ensure the equality and dignity of every member of the society in the eyes of social security, and raise the authority of the latter in the society.

Secondly, we should clearly define the ownership of the property right of the social insurance fund, i.e. it belongs to all the insurers, while the ownership of individual insurance funds belong to the insurers themselves. Strictly observing this principle we should seek to unite and coordinate the three components which comprise this insurance system: a) the individual worker (staff), b) the enterprise and c) the management organs of social security.

China is a developing country and economic development is its central task. The question of social security can be truly solved only by highly efficient economic development. Therefore, we must correctly treat the relations between equity and efficiency in the reform of the social security system. We must also clearly and definitely realize that: Equity means fairness and equal opportunity, not the egalitarian "eating from the same big pot." We can by no means try, in the name of equity, to maintain so-called "high-level security" which exceeds the level of economic development. We do not want social security become the "shelter" for "feeding the lazy." The principle of "efficiency first but giving consideration to equity" must be thoroughly carried out under the conditions of market economy.

Chapter VI
Legislation in China's Economic Transformation

New legislation must be provided which will serve as a basis for steady economic gains in the period of transition leading to a market economy. The problem is that this legislation must take as a precondition, the necessity of reform.

I. The Coordination of Reform and Legislation

The smooth coordination of reform and legislation will successfully bring us through this transition period to the market economy.

Market economy is after all the legally sanctioned economy. The establishment and improvement of the market economic system must be standardized and ensured by a complete legal framework. In recent years, China has speeded up economic reform and the Chinese market economy now has developed sufficiently to require further legislation.

The matters which must be dealt with are:

1) Property ownership. Today, this subject occupies a very important and critical position in China's reform. Without a thorough clarification and firm legal definition concerning such issues, including company's property right, individual property and the private property right, in the rapidly growing modern enterprise system the transition to a true market economy will be greatly hampered.

2) Market relations. In our daily lives we can find many

examples in temporary regulations or administrative orders concerning economic affairs that run counter to the basic principles of a market economy and show the lingering characteristics of a planned economy. Therefore, equal competition must be defined as the basic principle in the transition towards market economy.

3) Social relations. A large number of ordinary people are concerned about or support the reform in China's transition to market economy, because the reform has a direct connection with their economic social benefits. Ordinary people in China have received tremendous rewards from the past ten years of reform. They support the reform, but they often show more concern about their benefits from the reform. Therefore, the strengthening of social security legislation to protect people's new social relations in the market economy and insure fair distribution of social benefits is an important issue in promoting the development of the market economy and to guarantee social stability.

4) Coordinate relations. In the transition from the planned economy to a market economy, "going to court" has become a very common phenomena and it is quite normal to find officials and civilians engaged in law suits. But since our legal system is not comprehensive, in such circumstances, it is of prime importance to speed up the drafting and passage of legislation in basic procedures in the market economy. Without exactly established procedures there would be no law and order. This is particularly important today. Most problems which occur in daily life have two sides. Both parties have their reasons and justifications for their actions. But too often whoever has the greater power can get away with doing what he likes, and whoever has the greatest advantage can continue to do things in his own way without regard to laws or standard procedures. But the law must be impartial. Today, promulgating exact legislation and then enforcing such legislation are both very important issues. Legislation must be adaptable to the new situation of the reform. Legislation for the socialist market economy is badly needed. On the one hand, laws for normal economic activities should be worked out as soon as possible. On the other hand, we must realize that the establishment of a complete market economy has been taken on

as a long term goal and there are still major issues which haven't been solved. What's more, there are still some different opinions on some of the major issues.

In view of the above-mentioned facts, there are two most important issues that must be guaranteed by legislation on an immediate basis. First, the legal private property rights should be protected by law. And secondly, the market environment must be protected during this time of transition to prevent unnecessary intervention from every side especially state and local administrative intervention.

In order to meet the needs of the transition, we must allow and support local administrative organs to enact their own legislation.

During the transition towards the market economy, there is a disequilibrium problem and it will last for a long period of time. So we must encourage and support the local practice of legislation as well as that of coastal opening area and special economic zone, and give them more legislative power in order to reach the goal of allowing some areas with favorable conditions to get rich first. This is reality in China, particularly during the transition.

The reform of the government management system must shift the emphasis from mainly direct adminstrative control to economic and legal control.

In speeding up the transition towards the market economy, the government behavior is of prime importance. In the planned economy of the past, you did everything on government orders. You produced everything based on government decisions. But a market economy operates on a different basis. Here enterprises can determine their own form of management, and gear production in the economic profits according to market requirements. Thus, the government must change its function. In strengthening the mechanics of macro reform, we've suggested reforms in the monetary system, finance and taxation system, investment system, foreign currency system and foreign trade system. With these in operation our macroeconomic regulation and control will work within the principles of the market economy and lay a very important foundation for the overall economic development of the country.

Countries have evolved their own ways to realize macroeconomic control, but it must be done within the framework of a market economy. A socialist market economy must also accomplish this in order to establish needed regulations and control.

But because China is a society that has traditionally ruled by direct administrative orders, and such a system is so deeply planted, that even today administrative measures are still used to regulate and control the economy.

The most fundamental problem in the transition to the market economy is the reformation of this old macro-control system and to standardize macroeconomic regulation and control, and to establish the legal system of socialist market economy.

II. We Must Make Use of Advanced Legislation in the Transition of the Economic System

A modern market economy has its basic principles. And these have been collected up in many parts of the world and passed into law as advanced economic legislation. Making use of the legislation and adapting it to our own objective situations will be beneficial in advancing our own economic reform by enabling us to better conform to the principles of the market economy system. The law of market economy has no national boundaries. It is applicable to every country in the world.

Market economy has its universal law and general character. It is a kind of self regulating mechanism which allocates resources and distribute social labor forces based on the law of value, the law of competition and the law of supply and demand. These three laws are the basic laws of a market economy. Any attempt at establishment and development of a market economy system will go nowhere if these are not permitted to hold sway.

Aside from these key laws, there are also other requirements for the modern market economic system. The main body of the market economy requires independence, equality, and the openness and impartiality of competition. It requires the principles of self-government, free contract, making compensation for equal value, honest credit, freedom from arbitrary penalty for mistakes, protection of the rights and interests of the consumers and the inviolability of the civilians' private properties. It also requires a sound market system, improved social security, necessary macro control and conformation to the international market. As the market economy develops and expands internationally, we will see that it will be governed by no national boundaries. The rules of market economy are applicable to all countries. Whenever the market economy is established and developed, the normal laws and the basic requirements must be followed.

The development of the market economy has a history of several hundred years. The legislation of the market economy has developed along with the development of the market economy. It has gone through constant adjustment, revision, abolition and re-establishment in order to suit the objective requirements and development of a market economy. Contemporary market economic legislation summarises the basic patterns found in the course of the long-term development of market economy. It also summarises the historic experience of the countries in particular the Western developed countries which adopted the market economic mold in the running of their economies. Because of the openness and exchanges among the countries, countries of the world have to learn from each other in economic legislation. In general this is a tendency, in countries with market economy, to draw experience from each other, learn from each other, even mix their experiences together (including non-market economic experience) to formulate new procedures that further advance the market economic system. For instance, in modern market economy the adequate intervention by the government, the planning guidance, and social welfare, have all, to some extent, learned from the planned economic system. So we could say, the basic legislation of the contemporary market economy manifests the fundamental laws of human history. It is a common achievement of human civilization, recorded into law, which can be used by all countries in the world in developing their own market economies.

By making use of and adapting to the advanced legislation in the world market economy the transition from traditional economy to the market economy in China will be speeded up. Practical experience indicates that the great economic achievements made by the Western developed countries have a lot to do with their relatively mature legal systems. Such systems suit the market economy with their strict rule by law. In making full use of and adapting this advanced legislation, China will not only establish her market economy right away, but also avoid making the same mistakes made earlier by others. In this way China's market economy will develop in a direct way from its current conditions to full maturity and modernization. And in doing so it will be taking a short cut.

To create the appropriate legal environment through making use of and adapting to the world's advanced economic legislation is not only necessary for China's further opening but also one of the responsibilities required by GATT and regional economic co-operation.

As China is further opening to the outside world and regional economic co-operation is strengthened, its economy will become more and more internationalized. On the one hand, the economic internationalization requires a unity of structure. But behind this, a corresponding legal basis and system is necessary as a protection and guarantee. The idea is not to make this a self-protecting legal system. It must be an open legal system which fits international standards and international market economic requirements. It must link up the common international practices. At present, China's opening to the outside world does not enjoy an ideal legal environment. This brings certain difficulties and inconveniences for foreign investors. We have no choice but to imrpove this situation and bring conditions up to international standards. China's conclusion of more bilateral and multilateral agreements as well as international treaties with foreign countries, and strengthening regional economic co-operation, especially China's return to GATT will find it necessary to establish a market economic system and a foreign trade operational mechanism which are in accord with the international norms. And China's market economic legislation must observe international agreements and fulfil the obligations of international treaties.

Our socialist market economic legal system must be established according to China's reality. Making use of and adapting to the market economic legislation of the countries and regions concerned China should proceed from its own economic development strategy and requirements involved in becoming part of worldwide integration.

China must further open to the outside world, actively take part in international competition and cooperation and keep up with the world market in order to realise its strategic economic goals and objectives in the 21st century. To meet these targets, the legislation of China's market economy must try to be scientific, modern and internationalized. At the moment, to keep up with the ever increasing international economic contacts and with speeding up of the processes of regionalization and integration of the world economy, more and more countries and regions are attaching great importance to revising and reshaping their laws. In learning from other countries, we should pay attention to the following problems:

—Universality. We must choose and introduce the economic legislation which reflects the basic law of market economy and general international characteristics.

—Modernization. When learning from and adapting to the legislation of market economy, we must choose internationally advanced law system and regulations of market economy to promote the modernization of China's market economic legal system to ensure the fast development of socialist market economy.

—Internationalization. In learning from and adapting to legislation concerning the market economy, we must give full consideration to the internationalization of China's economy. It will be beneficial to China to open wider to the outside world, to engage in international economic and trade activities, to strengthen regional economic cooperation, to link up to the international market and to co-ordinate directly with international economic bodies.

—Systematizing. The market economic system and operation mechanism are an integrated system. All the systems in the market economy are inter-related, interdependent and inter-restricted. In the use of and adaptation to the world market economic legislation we have to ensure the coordination and dovetail of the reform, and the complete unity of a socialist market economic system.

—Compatibility. In making use of and adapting to foreign laws, we should adopt good advice from all quarters, take in the most outstanding and rational regulations of the market economy, follow the generality and universal law of market economy, continuously consolidate the native law.

There are some identical points as well as distinct differences between our socialist market economy and the market economies of the other countries and regions. Therefore, in learning from and adapting the legislation of the world's market economies we must keep in mind our own needs and specific existing situations.

Along with the return of Hong Kong and Macao to the motherland and the ever expanding economic relations across Taiwan Straits, the economic integration of the Chinese nation will be the general trend. Priority should be given to learning from the experience of economic legislation in Hong kong and Taiwan to promote the formation of a coordinated system and a common market of the Chinese economy.

1) The laws in Hong Kong and Taiwan represent the laws of the world's market economy, so they have important value as a reference point in the process of adaptation.

To form a coordinated system and a common market of the Chinese nation, we must have not only a common economic system but a correspondingly interactive legal system that will, insofar as possible, minimize regional clashes and obstacles. With this in mind the mainland should actively learn from the economic legislation of Hong Kong and Taiwan and work to build up the necessary legal environment.

After Hong Kong and Macao return to China in this century, there will be a situation of "one country with many laws." This situation cannot help but spur mutual cooperation and coordination between the different areas.

2) In learning from and adapting to the economic legislation of Hong Kong and Taiwan we must pay attention to solving some specific issues. These include the fact that the fundamental social system on the mainland is different from that of Hong Kong and Taiwan; that the law systems of the mainland and Taiwan belong to a continental legal system although Taiwan has also adpoted some points from the American and British systems while Hong Kong law falls entirely within British and American legal frameworks. These differences mean different legal concepts and different terminology. Moreover, Hong Kong is practiced a specialized economic structure known as a free port, while Taiwan is characterized as an island economy. They are both different with that of the mainland. So economic legislation of Hong Kong and Taiwan won't be totally introduced.

3) International economic practice itself is a product of commodity economy and market economy. It is a code for participation in international markets. Because of this, if China wants to take an active part in the international division of labour, participate in international markets, improve its investment environment, introduce more foreign investment and advanced technology and management experience, solve impartially and rationally the legal disputes and problems which have arisen in the economic exchanges with foreign countries, it must be familiar with international practices and act according to them. These international practices form our link to international economic contacts and the world markets. Since there are great differences in the legal systems between the mainland, Hong Kong and Taiwan, the mainland's legislation will never completely follow the legal systems of Hong Kong and Taiwan. So in economic cooperation between the mainland and Hong Kong and Taiwan obstacles and conflicts will be inevitable. The best way to remove these obstacles and conflicts is to strictly follow the international practices concerning economic exchanges and corporations. Law on Economic Contracts Involving Foreign Interests issued in 1985 and the General Regulations of Civil Law promulgated in

1986 stated clearly: In the event that the law of the People's Republic of China and the international treaties to which China did not join, do not clearly specify, it is the international practice that will be applicable. This has established the legal basis for the mainland to observe international practices in economic exchanges with foreign countries. But what is more important at the moment is to extensively introduce international practices into the legislation of market economy. The facts show that as an international free port, Hong Kong's legislation has absorbed a lot from international practices. Because of its early involvement in the division of labour and cooperation in international markets, Taiwan's legislation reflects in certain aspects of international practice. So in order to strengthen the economic co-ordination and exchanges between the mainland, Hong Kong, Macao and Taiwan, the mainland must introduce more and more international practices into its legislation, adopt general international methods and adhere to internationally standard codes of behaviour in its relations with Hong Kong, Macao and Taiwan.

III. Start a Program of Trial Legislation in the Localities

One law may not apply to every circumstance. It can apply in specific circumstances. Because different countries have different social systems, different historic, cultural and geographic conditions, different economic foundations and different forms of government, all these factors create different situations and different problems. One view (existing historically and also in the present) is that, because of these pecularities, a law that applies to one area cannot be adapted by another.

A contrary view, however, holds that according to historical experience adaptation of laws from one region to another happens a great deal. Some successful examples are the adaptation of Roman Law by European countries and the adaptation and absorption of the Continental Law and the British, American laws by Japan.

There have also been some failed attempts. The endeavors of

Turkey to copy the French Civil Code in 1922 and Ethiopia's bid to adapt the Swiss Civil Code in 1982 were both in vain.

Therefore, in preparation for the adaptation of law, one needs to do earnest and careful investigation and research work, carry out feasibility studies, propose specific operating methods, continuously carry out tests and make any necessary revisions and modifications to ensure the success of the adaptation.

To reduce and even eliminate the potential risks and costs that could accompany the introduction of new laws, legislative trials and pilot projects should be strongly promoted in the localities.

If an attempted implementation of a new law fails, it inevitably impacts adversely on China's reform and opening-up. This is not conducive to China's quick transition to the market economy. To avoid risks of law adaptation and to reduce the cost of this program, we should wait for the experience gained in these limited legislative trials before attempting to institute them broadly throughout the country.

All provinces, municipalities and autonomous regions in China already have certain legislative powers endowed them by the state and can enact local laws and regulations insofar as they do not contradict with any national statutes. In particular, coastal areas and SEZs should fully use this power to adapt legislation to enhance their own economic growth.

Specific coastal opening areas and economic zones should be chosen to engage in tests to adapt certain laws. The framework of a socialist market economic system has been initially established in Special Economic Zones which are now more developed and as such more able to absorb and adapt advanced market economy legislation.

However, in some cases existing legislative power will prove insufficient and will need to be strengthened in the experimental areas. Hainan is the largest special economic zone in China and therefore the most suitable for testing the adaptation of new laws. Because of the more flexible legislative powers given Hainan by the National People's Congress, the province is now able to enact its own local laws and regulations.

图书在版编目(CIP)数据

中国经济转轨中若干改革问题研究:英文/迟福林著.—北京:
外文出版社,1997
(中国市场经济研讨丛书)
ISBN 7-119-01976-7

Ⅰ.中… Ⅱ.迟… Ⅲ.经济体制改革—研究—中国—英文
Ⅳ.F121

中国版本图书馆 CIP 数据核字(96)第 20132 号

责任编辑 吴灿飞
封面设计 唐 宇

中国经济转轨中若干改革问题研究

迟福林 著

★

© 外文出版社
外文出版社出版
(中国北京百万庄大街 24 号)
邮政编码 100037
北京外文印刷厂印刷
中国国际图书贸易总公司发行
(中国北京车公庄西路 35 号)
北京邮政信箱第 399 号 邮政编码 100044
1997 年(大 32 开)第 1 版
(英)
ISBN 7-119-01976-7 /F·37(外)
02150
4-E-3158P